52 Ways to Live the COURSE in MIRACLES

Cultivate a Simpler, Slower, More Love-Filled Life

Karen Casey

Conari Press

This edition first published in 2016 by Conari Press, an imprint of Red Wheel/Weiser, LLC

With offices at:
65 Parker Street, Suite 7
Newburyport, MA 01950
www.redwheelweiser.com

ISBN: 978-1-57324-684-2

Library of Congress Cataloging-in-Publication Data

Names: Casey, Karen.
Title: 52 ways to live the Course in miracles : cultivate a simpler, slower, more love-filled life / Karen Casey, PhD.
Other titles: Fifty two ways to live the Course in miracles
Description: Newburyport, MA : Conari Press, 2016.
Identifiers: LCCN 2016019826 | ISBN 9781573246842 (5.5 x 8.5 tp : alk. paper)
Subjects: LCSH: Course in miracles. | Spiritual life. | Meditations. | Casey,
  Karen.
Classification: LCC BP605.C68 .C373 2016 | DDC 299/.93--dc23
LC record available at https://lccn.loc.gov/2016019826

Cover design by Jim Warner
Cover photograph Light at the End © diephosiMore / Getty Images
Interior by Frame25 Productions
Typeset in Minion Pro

Printed in Canada

MAR

10 9   8 7 6 5 4 3 2 1

52 Ways to Live the COURSE in MIRACLES

I want to dedicate this book, first and foremost, to my husband Joe, who has been traveling this path with me for nearly forty years. We have been course students for more than thirty of those years, and he is my most loving teacher, on a daily basis.

I also want to dedicate it to all the fellow travelers who walk with us on this most inspired journey. Every day I thank the Holy Spirit for Helen Schucman's willingness to be the scribe. Had she said no or ignored the call Jesus made to her, we'd all have suffered until someone else said, "I will."

And to all of my friends who sit with us in our home every Monday, reading and sharing our thoughts on the message Jesus has sent us, I say, Thank you. You have made the journey so much more meaningful.

And last, I want to acknowledge all those individuals who have read my first book on the course, *Daily Meditations for Practicing the Course,* and continue to reach out to me on a daily basis. We are students, one and all. And I thank you for walking this journey with me.

Nothing real can be threatened. Nothing unreal exists.
Herein lies the peace of God.

Contents

Introduction   xi

1. Love is letting go of fear.   1

2. Every loving thought is true. Everything
else is an appeal for healing and help.   6

3. Wherever we are is the next perfect place to be.   10

4. No experience is lacking in purpose.
Every encounter is holy.   13

5. Forgiveness is the key to peace.   16

6. Every experience is an opportunity
to live more peacefully.   20

7. What we see is what we choose to see.   23

8. When others are not kind, they
are afraid. Be kind anyway.   27

9. Don't let the mood swings of
others determine who you are.   31

10. Refrain from seeing oneself
as being unfairly treated.   34

11. Every experience is the next
perfect lesson with the right partner.   37

12. No one is where he is by accident,
and chance plays no part in God's plan.   40

13. Every person we encounter
    is one of our learning partners.   43

14. We cannot change the world, but
    we can change our minds about the world.   47

15. Anger is the all too common mask for fear.   51

16. Would you rather be peaceful or be right?   55

17. Grasp fully this moment only and discover peace. 59

18. We have access to two voices in our minds.
    Which one will we listen to?   63

19. The world we see is a witness to our state of mind. 67

20. To shift your state of mind, make the choice
    to be loving regardless of the situation.   71

21. Every word uttered is coming from
    a place of love or a place of fear.   75

22. The Holy Spirit has every answer we need.   78

23. Every encounter is a holy encounter.   81

24. Forgiveness is our primary assignment
    in this life, and the key to our happiness.   84

25. When one door closes, another opens.
    God has a better opportunity for us.   88

26. Don't let the past define the present.   92

27. Everyone is a messenger.   96

28. Being gentle is our pathway to peace.
When the journey began, most of us
had no idea what was in store for us.   100

29. Acceptance is the doorway to discovering peace.   104

30. A miracle is a simple shift
in perception. Nothing more.   107

31. We decide the world we want
to see and then we create it.   111

32. There is no struggle too big to relinquish.   115

33. Your mission is simple: live lovingly.   119

34. We are here only to be truly helpful.   123

35. Choosing the Holy Spirit as your constant
companion promises a peaceful journey.   127

36. If the thought you are protecting wouldn't
please God, exchange it for one that would.   131

37. The hovering angels that never leave our side
are giving us comfort and protection. Just look to
them for your every need. Begin today.   135

38. Not one of the illusions you
made replaces the truth.   139

39. The separation never occurred.   143

40. Our thoughts are all that can hurt us.   147

41. Remember that the Holy Spirit, the
Voice, is the Answer, not the question.   151

42. The Holy Spirit will take what the ego makes
and transform it into a learning opportunity.   155

43. The ego was made without love.
The Holy Spirit knows only love.   159

44. Our willingness to join with others reduces
our fear and gives inner peace a chance—the
peace that will eventually change this planet.   163

45. As egos, we see only what we want to see.   167

46. Christ's vision allows everyone who
is willing to see others without judgment.   171

47. The Holy Spirit translates the laws of God.   175

48. To have peace we must teach it.
Only then do we learn it.   179

49. God did not leave us comfortless even though we
"chose" to leave Him and our home in Heaven.   183

50. No call to God will ever be
unheard or unanswered.   187

51. We do not walk alone. God's angels are
hovering all around us, now and forever.   191

52. You will be told what God wills for you each
time there is a choice to make. Go in peace
from this moment on.   195

Concluding Thoughts   199

Acknowledgments   205

Introduction

The impact *A Course in Miracles* has had on my life is nearly immeasurable. I was first introduced to the course in 1981. I was five years sober at the time and hung on to Alcoholics Anonymous like my life depended on it. Which, of course, it did. But I was also yearning for something more, something that might quiet my near-constant anxiety.

I was one of those people who, from my first introduction to AA in 1976, went to multiple meetings a week. But I still longed to feel the quiet, secure connection to "a higher power" that so many of my friends quite obviously had. I simply had not found that connection to be very sustainable. At a meeting and while with friends at the meeting following the meeting, I'd be quite content. Then I'd go home. What I had been feeling seemed to flee the moment I walked through the door of my own apartment.

And that dis-ease, which took me to the brink of suicide more than once, subsequently hounded me into writing my first book, *Each Day a New Beginning: Daily Meditations For Women*, which has been followed by more than two dozen other books over the last thirty-four years. While in the act of writing, God, as I understand God, always shows up. But I have had long dry spells of not sitting in the quiet of my study listening to the inner voice and writing all that I hear. During those dry spells my frantic mind searches for solace. For connection. Historically, I did not, and often still don't, even with more than forty years sober, feel the presence of God when I'm not at a meeting or writing.

Some would no doubt say, "But how lucky you are. Your anguish has made you a published writer." And while that is true, the emptiness I have so often felt becomes nearly intolerable. And scary. For decades I prayed for more than the flimsy connection I occasionally felt to a power outside of myself. And then a sister-in-law sent me *A Course in Miracles*.

It was a three-book set at that time, and I had no idea which book to read first. I picked up the text and read the introduction about how the course came to be. That comforted me, but when I tried to read the text that followed, I felt overwhelmed. Even though I had a PhD I couldn't, with ease, grasp the spiritual message. It seemed unnecessarily complicated. I was looking for a fix that could quiet my troubled mind. And heart.

I chose to tackle the workbook first. It wasn't really much easier, but the lessons, one for each day of the year, gave me a structure—one not dissimilar from the daily meditation book I had been writing at that time. The workbook felt doable. So my journey with *A Course in Miracles* began, and it has never ceased. In fact, I can say with certainty that my commitment to the study of *A Course in Miracles* will continue until that day when my journey in this illusion has ended.

I love *A Course in Miracles*. It offers me a moment-by-moment reprieve from my ego so long as I turn to the quieter inner voice for my next thought. As the course tells us, *the ego always speaks first; it is loudest and it is always wrong.* The Holy Spirit never leaves one's mind, but it waits to be sought out for the next best response to any situation we are confronted with. What a quiet blessing the Holy Spirit is. Never pushy, but always present. It has walked me through myriad difficult situations. It will continue to be the loyal companion that promises peace instead of this, *whatever this is.*

Writing a book of essays about the course, suggesting how one can practice it for personal benefit, is so pleasurable. Every word I write is a constant reminder of how to cultivate greater peace in my own life. What could be better than that? Nothing comes to mind, frankly.

My intent is to take you on a journey through fifty-two simple ideas, offering you not only an explanation of the idea but also proof of how helpful and practical each idea really is through sharing some of my own experiences. I have also created an affirmation for each entry that will nurture you and strengthen your peace of mind. And what more can any of us really desire than a peace-filled mind?

My life has gradually been changed by the course. Little by little, day by day, I have become quieter. I have grown in my trust that there is a kinder, softer way to live. I am able to appreciate the many encounters I have every day, knowing that each one of them has come because of a lesson I have sought. And best of all, with the help of the course, I am able to feel nurtured by lesson after lesson because the Holy Spirit is translating it for me. Helping you translate your experiences is the intention of this book. Helping you enjoy greater peace is my heart's sole desire.

There isn't one "perfect" way to read and utilize this book. You may want to review the many essay titles and read them according to what strikes your fancy. Some of you will want to read it from cover to cover immediately. Many will want to take the book in smaller doses so that you can actually practice incorporating the ideas in your daily encounters. Whatever makes sense to you makes sense! It's about you making the changes in your perspective, and thus your behavior, that will guarantee greater peace moment by moment.

Why does this even matter? Only one reason comes to mind from my perspective. Nurturing greater peace within ourselves will benefit the multitudes who walk this planet with us. The ripple effect won't skip anyone. *Not a single person.* And what this means is that each one of us who is determined to meet our contemporaries, our friends, our neighbors, the strangers among us, and even those few we may consider enemies with love and acceptance will have impacted the 7 billion who live here too in ways we can only smile about.

The question is: Are you up to the task? Are you ready to be counted as a peacemaker? If the answer is yes, turn to essay one and begin.

My love goes full force out to each one of you as you attempt to make your mark. As Margaret Mead said so many years ago, "Never doubt that a small group of thoughtful, committed citizens can change the world. Indeed, it is the only thing that ever has."

Chapter 1

Love is letting go of fear.

M ore than thirty-five years ago, I was introduced to the spiritual principle "love is letting go of fear" through a book by that name written by Dr. Gerald Jampolsky. I knew nothing about *A Course in Miracles* at that time, but the idea that the connection between love and fear, a very core idea in *A Course in Miracles,* needed to be reckoned with got my attention. Dr. Jampolsky was best known then as the founder of the Center for Attitudinal Healing, a program he started in Marin County, California, in the mid-1970s that brought comfort and spiritual healing to children suffering from cancer.

I was particularly drawn to Jampolsky's writing style. His message was gentle. Very healing. Easily accessible. And extremely practical. The crux of his small book was about changing one's mind, thus making it possible to live from a place of love rather than being controlled by fear. His twelve simple principles seemed revolutionary to me.

I didn't have any idea when I read his book that Jampolsky was a devotee of *A Course in Miracles* or that his words would guide me to becoming a student of the course a short time later, but indeed that was the journey I embarked on. And what a journey it has been.

I'd have to say that nearly every spiritual perspective I now cherish is one that has been influenced by something I read either in the 669-page text, the 488-page workbook, or the 92-page manual for teachers that comprise *A Course in Miracles*. I'm so grateful for the vision I am now guided by. It's a simple vision. It's a practical vision. And it's a gentle vision, not unlike the one I was so comforted by when I read *Love Is Letting Go of Fear* more than thirty-five years ago.

Living life in the simple lane appeals to me. And there is nothing quite as simple as recognizing that every expression, every word, and every action any one of us makes is motivated by one of two feelings: *love or fear*. When I was first introduced to this idea, I scoffed. Surely people's behavior was more complicated than that. Indeed, I was certain mine was. And then I was helped by the readings in the course, coupled with long discussions with other course students, *A Course in Miracles* workshops, and books by Marianne Williamson, Kenneth Wapnick, and Jon Mundy, to see how much less complicated most of us really are.

Fear absolutely motivates people to be angry, sullen, dismissive, and, far too often, cruel. It can also initiate violence in myriad forms. Cable news, minute by minute, alerts us to the most recent evidence of fear in action. In families and between countries. In our neighborhoods and among folks we will never meet.

Fear is powerful. And all-pervasive at times. With some individuals it seems unending too. My own dad fell into this category. I'm pretty certain he would have insisted that he loved my siblings, my mother, and me; however, his love felt compromised, very conditional. And most of the time he was tense and quick to anger. Perhaps something had happened at work that upset him. Or maybe one of my siblings left a bike in the driveway. Something big or minor could have triggered the rage. But the repercussions were always registered at home. Always. Quite often at the supper table.

It wasn't until years later, after I was encouraged to interview him for a class assignment about family origins, that I came face to face with who my dad really was. My simple question, "Will you tell me about your life?" resulted in the reply, "I have been afraid every single day since I was six years old." He told me he had accidentally cut off two of his younger brother's fingers with the old push lawn mower and was severely punished for it. Trying to be perfect, in every way, from that moment forward instilled a fear that simply couldn't be quelled. He was tormented by it until the day he died.

I was stunned. My dad, afraid? He always seemed so confident. What I didn't understand then, but eventually learned from my *Course in Miracles* teachers, was that anger is only one of the many masks hiding fear. Let me be clear. My dad was angry. Often. But finally realizing that fear had precipitated his anger was eye-opening.

The only sane response to someone else's fear, regardless of how it is being manifested, is to be loving.

I was relieved to finally learn my dad's truth, but so sad for him that life had been so difficult. His near-constant struggle, of course, made life a struggle for all of us. That's what fear does. It gets projected onto others, thus controlling the dynamic between all the people present. The dance our family did was anything but a smooth waltz.

I've studied long and hard, read and reread *A Course in Miracles* in its entirety many times, in fact, in order to be able to "occasionally" appreciate that the only sane response to someone else's fear, regardless of how it is being manifested, is to be loving. An expression of love is the only thing that will pave the way for freedom from the awful sting of fear that is being expressed in any person's anguished behavior.

Making the choice to be loving, difficult though it may be, isn't actually as hard as it may initially sound. I'm reminded of Mother Teresa's gentle admonition to "be kind to everyone and start with the person standing next to you." Making a decision to be kind or loving can happen with little or no planning. You just do it. You smile. You offer help. You remember that we, each one of us, are on assignment to be helpful to one another. That's all. That's absolutely all. It's quite enough, actually.

I will choose to be loving and kind in
every encounter I experience today. My
own spirit will be lifted every time I try to
lift the spirit of someone else.

Chapter 2

Every loving thought is true.
Everything else is an appeal
for healing and help.

This principle is profound. Deeply profound, I think. What it means is that any thought we hold that isn't loving is actually a cry for help. *Yes, any thought.* Those sneaky, quiet judgments; the unspoken put-downs; even our negative recollections about someone are all—*all*—cries for help. What I say to you or about you mirrors who I am, loud and clear, in that moment. And when I am saying or thinking something that is not kind, I am in trouble. Personally and spiritually in trouble. And I need help.

How twisted our thinking becomes when we are afraid, when we are feeling less than others or perhaps even more than someone else. The fact of the matter is, what I am saying or thinking about you actually isn't about you at all. It's about me. My thoughts or words perfectly reflect what I am thinking about myself in that very moment. This truth can oftentimes feel ugly. Any truth we don't like we'd prefer to deny. Or project onto someone else. That's the human side of us. Let's not be ashamed, however. Let's accept who we are in the moment so that we can become who we'd rather be in the next moment.

How do we live with this repugnant fact about ourselves? One of the first helpful things to acknowledge is that we experience two voices in our minds. Continuously and simultaneously. One is always loud, very negative, and quite destructive; and unfortunately, it speaks first. This is the ego's voice. It's the one responsible for our distasteful thoughts and actions.

The other voice we will hear, but only if we choose to hear it, is very quiet, very kind, very loving, and, most importantly, it speaks truth. This is the voice of the Holy Spirit, who is God's *representative* in this world of illusions that our egos have created.

Certainly, choosing to listen to the loving voice of the Holy Spirit within our minds is preferable. It is definitely the most sensible. However, because it generally isn't the first voice we hear, we get hijacked. And then sidetracked. So easily sidetracked. Thus, before we know it, we are passing judgment on, or worse, audibly criticizing, whomever is present. Of course, what we are thinking or saying isn't the truth about who is standing before us. We have already established that whatever has been uttered or thought reveals solely who we are. In that moment.

The hurt has been registered already, however, and it's a hurt whose impact ripples throughout the world. Quite obviously, it reflects back on us with as much vehemence as it projects forward. Instantaneously, the entire universe of souls has been touched by the ugly ego that commandeered our attention. That's the awful and yet awesome power of the butterfly effect. *What I say or do to you, I do to everybody.*

Our personal mission is holy: give only love.

Although we can't put this genie back in the bottle, we can recognize the error of our ways quickly and refrain from exaggerating the problem we have created. The best way to refrain, of course, is to quietly acknowledge to ourselves the shortcomings we have once again been held hostage by. Having two voices in our minds requires that we be vigilant. Constantly. The loudest voice is simply never the kindest. Nor is it ever loving. Consequently, we must make our amends, if they are called for, and move on. Just move on. The next moment and its opportunity are calling to us.

To repeat what has already been hailed as the message here, loving thoughts that give rise to loving actions are the life-sustaining activities in what appears, most often, to be a chaotic, dangerous universe. Our personal mission is holy: *give only love.* And we accomplish this by making the choice to listen to that quieter voice. Not only will we be changed entirely, but the picture before our eyes will change entirely too.

Indeed, only loving thoughts are deserving of us. Only loving thoughts coupled with loving actions are the gifts we must bestow on every soul we encounter. Being the example of truth at every turn transforms every moment of life. Your life and mine too.

※

Transforming my life is within my power.
It begins with a soft heart today.

Chapter 3

Wherever we are is the next perfect place to be.

How comforted I am by knowing that I am where I need to be right now. The same is true for you. This also means that where we were yesterday or forty years ago was where we needed to be then too. As the course, through the words of Jesus, reveals, there are no accidents. Every experience we have and every person we meet is fulfilling a part in our separate, though perfect journey.

My trajectory, and yours too, is divinely targeted. This doesn't mean we should not have felt the pinch of uncomfortable experiences at times. That these things should not have happened. On the contrary, they were necessary points on the learning curve that is actually intended to help us remember *who we really are.*

And who are we really? We are God's children who are still very much at home in Heaven. But the moment we mysteriously (could it have been mistakenly?) created the ego, we rebelled and imagined that we had escaped from Heaven. We were intent on ruling ourselves in our own "more perfect world."

Alas, in truth we didn't really leave God at all. Not really. We remain "at home" with Him right now even though we think we are in this madly insane world of illusions that our egos painstakingly created, one idol at a time.

Look around. The insanity of what the ego has made is nearly beyond belief. In the name of "God" people are killing one another in the vilest ways. The evening news is replete with tragedy. The 24/7 cable networks, with all their gory details, are suffocatingly oppressive. But we watch. And wring our hands. And say, What can be done? *And then we remember . . .*

What a blessing to remember that what we are watching isn't actually happening in the real world. So how does what we gaze upon fit into the principle that "wherever we are is the next perfect place to be?"

This question has intrigued me ever since that day more than three decades ago when I committed to a lifelong study of *A Course in Miracles*. If what we are seeing in our neighborhoods and on television isn't *real*, how do we explain it? And why should I, or you, believe that what the course says about this world, in contrast to the real world, is truth?

That quieter voice that always speaks truth helps us to lift our eyes above the fray, to seek the vision of Christ that is always present in every face.

With time—actually, lots of time—I have come to understand that being willing to believe the truth isn't a dilemma, not really. I have become satisfied with choosing to accept that this classroom, our world, is where violence and tragedy appear to be happening. This classroom is where we can see what the ego part of one's mind is capable of doing. The havoc is evidence of the insanity of the ego. With this as a backdrop, it's glorious to remember that the ego voice isn't the only voice present in our minds. Hallelujah.

That other, quieter voice that always speaks truth helps us to lift our eyes above the fray, to seek the vision of Christ that is always present in every face, regardless of the horrors of the violence. It's in this moment that *we are in the right place at the perfect time, serving to demonstrate for others that peace is always possible.* Always. It's in these moments that Spirit is calling us to be who we truly are: God's children, one and all.

There is no more perfect place to be. Ever.

I relish knowing that I am not, in actuality, part
of this insanity all around me. I am free.
I am free. Spirit is my guide.

Chapter 4

No experience is lacking in purpose. Every encounter is holy.

It might be difficult to believe that no experience is lacking in purpose after we've been fired from a job we thought was perfect for us. Or after a spouse has left us for another partner. However, we are always experiencing exactly what we need to experience at exactly the right time. Therefore, another career path or perhaps a new relationship must be heading our way. We have to trust that, in time, we will understand the holiness of whatever took us by surprise.

I feel such a sense of calm when I remind myself that every encounter I have with absolutely every person who engages me is for a reason. I don't need to know the reason, and I seldom do, immediately. But the experience will eventually be understood as one of the necessary puzzle pieces completing the picture of me.

When I gaze back over my life, recalling the dark periods along with the successes, I can see with clarity how each one of my experiences lent a thread or two to the tapestry that now describes me. The contrast between the bright colors and the dark ones gives depth to the picture that is still being woven, one encounter, one experience, one moment at a time. What is true for me is most certainly true for you.

All the mean happenings along with the glorious interludes made their mark for a reason. And each reason is sacred.

I was introduced to this idea many decades ago, although it didn't resonate with me then. The traumatic times surely weren't necessary, were they? The abuse, both emotional and sexual, could have been avoided. Wouldn't you agree? And yet hindsight has allowed me not only to understand the reasons for all those experiences, but I am actually able to celebrate each one of them for the contribution it has made to the package that is Karen today.

Each experience in my life prepared me to help at least one other person who was quite intentionally sent my way for the words of encouragement my survival could offer them. That's a beautiful way to make sense of our lives, I think. All the mean happenings along with the glorious interludes made their mark for a reason. And each reason is sacred.

I often wish I had known in my youth what I have learned to be true. I was a fearful child. A fearful teenager too. In all honesty, fear hounded me until I joined a twelve-step program in my mid-thirties. And it actually didn't leave for many years even then. I had no idea that who and what I was encountering were preparing me for the miraculous life I now enjoy.

Every life is miraculous. That is a fact that I now cherish. It's only when egos are in control that insanity reigns. And yet, in the midst of every insane act there is purpose, eventually. Perhaps the primary purpose is to show others that insanity need not reign if we listen to the softer, more loving guidance of the voice of the Holy Spirit. That presence never deserts us. Never. That presence can take any experience and wring the holiness out of it. My life is a testament of that. Yours too.

You and I are in the throes of
holiness today. It is carrying us to
our next perfect appointment.

Chapter 5

Forgiveness is the key to peace.

B ecause of the Internet's unstoppable news cycle, we are privy, nearly every day, to grieving parents whose children have been killed quite violently at the hands of others. And often we hear these same parents expressing their willingness to forgive the killers, a reaction that seems nearly unimaginable.

When the parents are asked how they can find it in their hearts to forgive such unspeakable crimes, they generally reply that not forgiving hurts more than forgiving. Hanging on to the anger or hate destroys them from within, and they can find no peace when revenge has made its home in their hearts.

Retribution certainly seems reasonable to many of us. Not so long ago, you could have counted me in this group. However, my developing spiritual education has offered me another perspective on a situation as grievous as the taking of a precious life. I have become willing to believe, although not without staunch resistance initially, that any act committed by someone that is not loving is actually a cry for help. A desperate cry for help.

Any act committed by someone that is not loving is actually a cry for help.

And every one of us makes that desperate cry for help too, far too many times a day. Perhaps our "crime" is a minor one, but it's still an unloving act. And that's a sure sign of a cry for help. According to the course there is no measurable difference between a major infraction and a minor one. *All unloving acts are considered equal, and all are cries for help.*

The even more important fact we must wrap our minds around is that all unloving acts are evidence of fear. Unadulterated fear. This fact, a well-defended truth within *A Course in Miracles*'s belief system, was not even remotely acceptable to me when I first became a student. I simply could not fathom, actually would not even consider, that rage, regardless of how it was being expressed, indicated fear. Fear, represented as a cry for help when it was being expressed so violently, so vehemently, was definitely a foreign idea to me. It wasn't until I became willing, little by little, to see it that way that I was moved to change my mind. I had always thought fear resulted in running away from a situation rather than facing it head-on in a mean or vicious way.

How I have changed! How extremely different is the perspective I now treasure so dearly. And with such relief, such peace of mind, I observe the egos of others acting out in ways I used to. Let me assure you, lest I be misunderstood, my change of mind didn't happen easily. Not at all. Maturity helped. Daily study helped. Prayer and meditation helped too. And reaping the benefits of being willing to see differently greatly helped. *But most of all*, truly seeking to listen to the quieter inner voice of the Holy Spirit cultivated the real change that has blessed my life. Every aspect of my life.

Being willing to forgive the actions of others, whomever those others are, knowing that what any one person does could be replicated by every other person too, almost moves me to tears. For certain it moves me to a quiet inner space, an inner space that sways to and fro in a peaceful way.

So much has changed in my life since I became willing to admit that no one of us is better than the worst of us, that we are one. *Indeed, we are one.* Even during those times when I can't wrap my mind around the truth of this idea, those instances when unspeakable acts are being committed by the strong against the weak, I have become willing to take a deep breath and say, "Yes, I am him; I am her. And we are worthy of forgiveness."

The forgiving heart is the balm that changes the winds of the universe. Nothing remains the same when any one person says, "I understand, I accept, I forgive. I love."

Peace will visit us today when we
acknowledge how alike we are to the least
of us. Forgiveness connects us as one.

Chapter 6

Every experience is an opportunity to live more peacefully.

This principle is powerful, uncompromising, and yet so simple. Nothing is left to chance. What is, is. Period. I love the finality, the strength, of a principle that shouts with such clarity. Don't you?

This principle helps me remember that *it's okay to exhale*. I don't need to hold my breath in anticipation of what might be just around the corner. I know, with total certainty, that whomever or whatever is about to greet me has come purposefully as the next opportunity I have been readied for. And the choice to accept whatever that experience is with a peaceful mind-set is mine to make. No one foists a choice on us. No one. Ever.

How I wish I had known this principle while yet a youngster. Or at least while struggling through my teens and early adulthood. I fretted over everything. In actuality, I worried myself sick on far too many occasions. Perhaps some of you can identify with this. I simply did not believe that a power of any sort was looking over my shoulder, offering protection of any kind. And today, I am quite convinced that hovering angels surround me wherever I am. What a difference a few short years have made. What a difference coming to believe in a powerful source of strength has made.

I have had my share of harrowing experiences. Most of us have. And particularly by the time one reaches seventy-six, we can be sure we have dodged a string of buses. But it tickles me to realize that even when it appeared a bus was headed right for me, not a single one of them was actually intended to hit me. Not one! What should happen does. Every time. What shouldn't doesn't. Every time.

A Course in Miracles states loud and clear: there are no accidents! One's journey is divine. One's journey is perfect. I remain amazed even after three decades of daily study that I can trust, moment by moment, that my experiences have been scripted. For me. Alone. Which means I need not be haunted by worry of any kind. *I will be watched over through every passageway I'm invited to traverse.* What can be better than that? Really nothing.

Not every experience in these past seventy-six years has been pleasurable, I can assure you. Many of them were painful. Some seemed extremely unfair. How can abuse of any form be necessary in one's divine journey, after all? But coming to believe that each experience played a crucial role in my life, teaching me an important lesson that was perfect for who I was to become, has allowed me to be extremely grateful for every experience that paid a visit.

Surviving ultimately means thriving.
We have been special teachers.

Because I know this has been true for me, I know it has also been true for you. The only reasonable response to this fact of our lives is to count ourselves lucky for the opportunities they have given us—opportunities that have allowed us to forgive even the unspeakable experiences, because forgiveness has given us the gift of peace, a peace that surpasses all understanding. We were chosen to receive our particular experiences. We were chosen so that we could then show others how even the unspeakable could be survived. Surviving ultimately means thriving. We have been special teachers. Very special way-showers. One and all.

Let us remember today that we are,
once and for all, teachers because of
what we have so luckily been taught.

Chapter 7

What we see is what we choose to see.

This is a pretty straightforward statement. One that actually comforts me now. But I still remember when I first encountered it as a student of *A Course in Miracles*. I was mystified by the word *chosen*. It implied that whatever I was looking at might not *really* be there at all, that it might actually be a figment of my imagination. The lack of certainty about this outer world of objects that my eyes gazed upon was unsettling.

Being patient hasn't been my strong suit. Even at my age I still want others to do my will when I will them to do so! I'm not proud of this, but I am willing to be begrudgingly honest. However, I have been teachable. And coming to believe, though a very slow process, that I project what I see is now a principle I accept as true. *True for you as well as for me, in fact.*

Seeing what we choose to see seems counterintuitive. Or so I thought when I was first embracing the course teachings. Why would anyone in their right mind choose to see death and destruction? Anger and abuse? Hate and vengeance?

And then I learned that seeing destruction—some act that was hurtful, evidence of rage, or even minor slights— were all examples of what the insane ego projected, and thus chose for me to see. Being able to embrace the idea that there were always two voices in my mind, one of them bent on creating some form of dis-ease, eventually brought relief. Eventually. And then coming to believe that the ego in the minds of others acted just as destructively explained why this world of bodies felt so very dangerous.

It's a huge and initially very difficult idea to accept that what we "see" happening around us isn't actually real; we are living in a classroom, one created solely by the ego. That the activities in this classroom aren't actually happening at all seems unfathomable to many. I heard this idea being discussed, explained, and confirmed hundreds of times in the study groups I went to before I surrendered to the idea. Peace of mind was the gift of finally coming to believe that the classroom was merely a teaching device.

Now I, like so many of my teachers, find great joy in reminding others that our difficulties, though seemingly real, are simply our opportunities to remember what we used to know for certain: *that we are still and always have been at home with God. We never really left. Our sojourn here has been an ego experiment, nothing more. Nothing less.*

I find it very comforting now to embrace the actual simplicity of *A Course in Miracles*. It surely didn't feel simple when I began this journey. It was my penchant for sticking with something that kept me reading and going to study groups. Nothing more than that. Most days, in the early years, I couldn't have explained to another soul what I had just read. Or heard. I simply trusted that when the time was right, I would grasp what I really needed to understand. I believed that the meaning was waiting for me.

What we need to understand about any experience or body of information will be revealed in the nick of time. What we don't yet need to understand lies dormant until the time is right.

I still believe that what we need to understand about any experience or body of information will be revealed in the nick of time. What we don't yet need to understand lies dormant until the time is right. Frankly, I treasure that idea. It keeps me from needlessly worrying. The phrase "more will be revealed," actually a direct quote from the Big Book of *Alcoholics Anonymous*, fits for *A Course in Miracles* too. We will understand what we need to understand when the time is right. And not a minute earlier. How much easier can God make it?

The really wonderful awareness that I have now, after being a student of the course for more than three decades, is that I see only what I choose to see, which means I can change the picture at will. With the help of the Holy Spirit, whose voice is as accessible as the voice of the ego, I can have the life I really want: one that is peace-filled and simply joyful.

Hallelujah!

I am on my way to changing my life today.
All in the blink of an eye. Are you?

Chapter 8

When others are not kind, they are afraid. Be kind anyway.

We are coming from a place of love or a place of fear with every thought we have, every action we take, every emotion that's either being expressed or lying dormant within us. It's a simple scorecard, actually. And remembering that every person we encounter is reflecting one emotion or the other helps us to choose the proper response. In all honesty, there is only one proper response. It's kindness. Regardless of the circumstances.

As mentioned earlier, Mother Teresa has been quoted as saying, "Be kind to everyone and start with the person standing next to you." I'm not positive she did say this, but it makes sense that she would. It also fits beautifully with the principles I hold so dear from *A Course in Miracles*. It takes the guesswork out of my repertoire of possible responses. There is never more than one that makes sense. And that one is loving-kindness.

The worry that so many of us are troubled with is quite often related to figuring out what to do in one situation or another. When we look at life from the simple perspective I'm suggesting here, it removes any need for worry. No matter who is crossing our path, be kind. No matter what problem they seem to have brought with them, be kind. No matter what a family member or neighbor might be doing that is beginning to get under our skin, pause and be kind. *No matter what, be kind.*

Growing up in a family where loud anger and silent retribution reigned didn't foster in me a desire to "simply be kind." I learned revenge. I wanted revenge. If not actual revenge, I at least wanted to fantasize about the revenge I'd visit on those who made me uncomfortable with their anger.

Paying someone back in kind was my motto. If you were mean to me, that was my invitation to be mean too. If you blamed me for something I clearly didn't do, I'd get you back. My way of looking at the world wasn't unique. Unfortunately. Payback is common. All too common.

Just turn on the evening news. Or any 24/7 cable network. Payback is the norm. From country to country, in one neighborhood after another, it keeps us in a downward spiral. A spiral that sucks the life out of hope. But we can turn this around. We can. Stepping off the escalator that's going down shows others that they too can step off. All it takes is one person to change the universe. One person who dares to stand up and decides to be a different example. An example of kindness.

All it takes is one person to change the universe.

Perhaps an idea like this seems too farfetched to even be worthy of consideration. However, from the perspective of *A Course in Miracles*, all it ever takes is one person to begin the change the universe is capable of accomplishing, because all of us together *are that one*!

To repeat again, for emphasis, what Margaret Mead said many years ago, way before *A Course in Miracles* had been scribed by Helen Schucman, "Never doubt that a small group of thoughtful, committed citizens can change the world. Indeed, it is the only thing that ever has."

And what is that small change one of us can instigate? Kindness. Simple kindness. Pass it on to whomever, wherever. Without giving a second thought to the situation. No matter what the circumstances are. Make the decision now, *right now*, that your response to the next person you encounter will be sincere kindness. Take note of his or her reaction when you can. Especially try to see what their next action toward another might be. Passing on that which we have received is the most common response. It's often called paying it forward. Not one of us is immune from this opportunity. Not one.

And you think you can't change the universe? I say, think again. You are its only possibility.

All we need to do today, or any day, is be an example of kindness. That's doing our part to change the world we share.

Chapter 9

Don't let the mood swings of others determine who you are.

This idea is one I didn't fully appreciate until I was in my forties. I had been introduced to it many years prior to my being able to incorporate it, however. In fact, it first came to my attention in 1971 because of a single line in John Powell's book *Why Am I Afraid to Tell You Who I Am?*: "Why should I let him decide what kind of day I am going to have?" This line was uttered by Powell's friend after being queried about his kindness to a very rude individual. I was stunned. I had always let others determine my day. My moment. My mind. Didn't I have to?

Being slow to shift how we see our world is normal. Many new ideas that become so very meaningful to us in time have to be walked around in for a while before we can put them on. And even after putting them on, we may have frequent missteps before actually adopting the idea as ours in everyday responses to the myriad happenings in our lives.

But no matter. False starts are a beginning, and that's really all we have to commit to, because the Holy Spirit will move right in and help us take the next step. In every instance. Indeed, everything in our lives is made easier because we have the constant companionship of God's emissary. Our part is simply to be willing to accept the help that is offered. Always offered.

Mood swings, ours and others', can create inner turmoil. Lots of it. Perhaps I've made the quiet response to them sound easy. Let me assure you, it's not initially easy. Old habits, ingrained responses, aren't easy to discard. Not at all. But I can promise you that this change is possible. I was the poster child for letting the behavior of others control how I thought, how I acted, and who I even thought I was. This is no longer true. And it hasn't been for more than a couple decades now.

What must we do if we want to avoid being controlled by others' moods? That's the question. And though the answer is simple, it's not easy. We must learn to step aside when someone else, *anyone else*, is hurling their nasty mood onto the unsuspecting universe of characters destined to encounter them. If we can visualize someone's mood as a fiery ball that has been thrown in our direction, we can more easily envision ourselves ducking or stepping out of the way of the oncoming object. *Actually taking a tiny step aside* in any tense situation, as a way of practicing this idea, will help you to see how effective such a simple act can be. Moving the body, even slightly, moves the mind. Moving the mind is how change is made real.

Moving the body, even slightly, moves the mind.
Moving the mind is how change is made real.

Changing ourselves is what this essay is proposing. We can't change others. Nothing about others is ours to change. But we can change who we are in situation after situation. We can change the thoughts we are willing to release; we can change the mind-set that has held us hostage for so long; we can change every single action we take. Every one of them. The big ones. The tiny ones. And with every one that we change, we are becoming more of the person God had intended us to be.

Perhaps you are wondering, Is this what my life has become? The hopeful answer is yes. We still have work to do. We still have lessons to learn. We still have people to meet. We still have changes to make, many of them, but the road before us is ours to chart, one thought, one action at a time. No one's mood swings ever need to hold us hostage again. No one's. The present is ours to live. The future is ours to create.

I am exactly where I need to be right now,
and whomever is before me has no
power over how I act or think or am.

Chapter 10

Refrain from seeing oneself as being unfairly treated.

Oh, the temptation is so great to feel unfairly treated. I know. That's who I was not so many years ago. From my experience, I'd dare to suggest we all might have carried that banner for a time. It was far easier than assuming responsibility for everything that had befallen us. Trying to make others responsible allowed us to pretend we were better than we thought we actually were. Our twisted thinking, of course, kept us stuck. Might still be keeping us stuck, and thus preventing us from growing in the very ways we are born to grow.

Alas, this no longer needs to be true. Whatever happened to us in the past we agreed to. Period. I know that sounds harsh. I resisted believing this for many years. How could I have agreed to the abuse? How could I have agreed to doing the many shameful acts I committed?

The fact that we have no memory of our agreed upon plan is what keeps the door open to our denial of the truth. But agree we did, as souls before waking up here in these bodies, in this classroom, in this world that is an illusion created by our egos.

*Whatever happened to us in the
past we agreed to. Period.*

Don't fret if this truth of who and what we are, who and what we did, seems more than you can grasp right now. We have all the time we need to embrace the truth of our journey here. But embrace it we must. Embrace it we will. Of this I am certain.

Since we can put to rest the idea that we were ever unfairly treated, how does this change what we need to accept about ourselves? When I grew comfortable with the idea that I honestly was a willing participant in every encounter I had, I experienced a relief that I hadn't counted on. The mystery of my many detours through life was solved. My journey had been divinely orchestrated, and I had been privy to each so-called detour before it was even experienced. Thus, there was no unfairness at all. What happened was as planned. What I learned was as planned. What I resisted was my own truth, which I would embrace. Eventually.

When we pause for a moment and look at our journey from this perspective, doesn't it all make sense? That's the conclusion I came to. There were no actual anomalies. Every person and every experience was part of the rhythm that became my song. Your song too. No two of us had *divined* the exact same melody, of course. But we did complement one another's song, and we will continue to make music for as long as our journey lasts. What a joyful realization.

Helping one another, by our own example, to embrace the truth that none of us were ever unfairly treated is surely one of the most important of all our agreed upon tasks in this classroom. And the best way to demonstrate this is to see the good in all our experiences. And to celebrate that good with all our companions. We are the teachers of one another. We are the students too. No one of us is the least of us. We are, in fact, one.

My life has felt so promising, so relevant ever since becoming a student of *A Course in Miracles*. The course principles have shifted how I see life (mine in particular), and the whole of us too. I am filled with a sense of peace that I had never imagined was possible as a troubled youngster. Even when I first discovered the course, I had no idea my life was about to change inexplicably. But it has, and *I can see clearly now*.

A simple thing like giving up the idea of "poor me" opens the door to a clarity and a peace of mind that is beyond our wildest dreams.

Chapter 11

Every experience is the next perfect lesson with the right partner.

How amazing the truth of this principle has been to my evolution as a spiritual being. I certainly didn't embrace this idea when I was first introduced to it. I simply couldn't fathom that every person I encountered was a "teacher" I needed to know. Far too many of them were people I wouldn't seek as friends today. But the whole of them, in retrospect, added to the tapestry that was becoming my life. Not one man or woman was inconsequential to who I was destined to be.

I now celebrate this journey that will continue to bring me in contact with those souls I need to know. In fact, those souls *I agreed* to know. Nothing in our lives is unexpected. Absolutely nothing. Perhaps we feel blindsided on occasion, but whatever and whoever comes our way is on assignment, an assignment we share.

I am completely comforted by this revelation, at long last. I may have a moment of doubt that *this too* I agreed to in a past long since forgotten; but as soon as I remember the truth of our journey in this classroom, I settle in, knowing that I am moving forward as planned.

Each choice any one of us makes has the potential of moving all of us forward.

Thinking of our encounters as providing the teachers and students we need in order to advance on this path allows me to feel privileged regarding the choices I get to make. Each choice any one of us makes has the potential of moving all of us forward, in the final analysis. What a breath of really fresh air. We live in concert with one another. The actual truth of the matter is that *we are one another*. We are a united whole. Not everybody resonates with this truth. Not yet, at least. It took me some time to wear the idea comfortably. But now, peace. A deep-seated peace has set in.

The best part of this principle is that it removes all concern about the journey, both where we are and where we are going. It's a "done deal," as they say. In actuality, we are simply along for the ride. The destination has been chosen and charted. Our job is to appreciate the scenery.

Does this course principle seem too farfetched to you today? Too unsettling? If it does, that's okay. Some ideas take longer for us to be comfortable with. They will wait for us, however. That's the truly comforting awareness I have had since becoming a student of *A Course in Miracles*. There is no timetable. I can move forward in my acceptance of the purposeful way my life is unfolding as slowly as I need to. The same is true for you. As Jesus so comfortingly tells us in chapter eight of *A Course in Miracles*, "If you want to be like me I will help you, knowing we are alike. If you want to be different, I will wait until you change your mind." How blessed we are. How very blessed we are.

There is truth. And nothing but the truth. When we are ready to accept it is up to us. We will be helped, however, by Spirit within. We are not on this path accidentally. We have not been introduced to these truths accidentally. There is nothing about our lives so far that is accidental. And tomorrow will prove to be no different.

Shouldn't we celebrate how peace-filled our lives can be? All we have to do is get on board with the principles being put forth in this book. We are divinely in charge of what comes next for us. We are divinely in charge of who we meet and where we go. We are divinely in charge of the pace we set. We are divinely present in one another's lives. We are Divine. Yes, Divine. So let's get over whatever resistance we have. It's only slowing down the journey to peace that we are here to make. The journey we are all making, in tandem and as one.

I won't get in my own way today. I'll cherish each encounter, remembering it is holy and intentional.

Chapter 12

No one is where he is by accident, and chance plays no part in God's plan.

There are no accidents in the evolution of our lives. That is a powerful statement, and it requires courage, strength, and humility to fully embrace it. It requires vigilance coupled with practice too. Lots of it. But when I am in touch with this truth, I feel such a sense of peace. Knowing that divine order is always commanding how life is unfolding removes me from the driver's seat. I am God's passenger in the limousine of life. And you are too.

It's surely common to forget how perfectly our lives are evolving. When any situation feels uncomfortable or when someone's behavior alarms us, it's easy to forget that the picture that is unfolding is according to a plan we simply haven't remembered to recognize as our truth in that moment. Being caught off guard by an unexpected occurrence doesn't make it wrong. We have merely forgotten that *what should happen does happen*. And when we pause and remember, we can breathe more easily once again.

How different my life would have felt had I been aware that every person's presence and each experience we were having was happening exactly as intended. I worried incessantly, both as a child and into adulthood, that I couldn't handle the experiences I seemed to wander into. To have been informed that no experience would ever invite me in that I had not been prepared for would have alleviated much anxiety, an anxiety that at times felt crippling.

Looking back now, I can see so clearly how inevitable each situation was and how, like the workings of a finely tuned Swiss watch, every aspect of my life, and your life too, has been weaving its way toward a future that has already been determined.

I've wondered, on occasion, if knowing that all was always well might have taken some of the joy that naturally accompanies an unfolding mystery out of my life. I don't know, of course. All I know for certain is that being joyful is one of the great gifts of being alive, and trusting that everything that's happening is part of the perfect plan for my life is accompanied by its own level of joy too—a peace-filled joy, as a matter of fact. It's safe to say that either way, knowing or not knowing, but trusting that all is well, promises the joy we deserve simply because we are God's children.

Does feeling angst about our lives serve any worthwhile purpose? I've concluded that if the practice of turning things over to the unseen greater power sets in motion a peace that sweeps away the angst, it has served a purpose. Anything that encourages us to seek a better way of seeing whatever is occurring is good because it strengthens a practice that initiates many rewards.

Wherever you are, wherever you go, whatever you do, you are ultimately fulfilling the perfect role you were uniquely created to fill.

It all comes down to this: wherever you are, wherever you go, whatever you do, you are ultimately fulfilling the perfect role you were uniquely created to fill. Although we have the choice, always, to take a detour or two, we will eventually find ourselves exactly where we were intended to be. There are no accidents. Remember? The dice has been rolled and the final destination awaits us. We will enjoy the perfect outcome, always. It may surprise us, and that's perfect too. The key is to relax and know that *all is well. All is always well.*

With both joy and quiet anticipation we can move forward, trusting implicitly that each day's journey is exactly what is intended.

Chapter 13

Every person we encounter is one of our learning partners.

W hat a beautiful thought it is to greet every person we encounter as a friend/teacher who has come to enlighten us about the very next thing we need to be aware of in our journey through life. The idea that no person we meet is superfluous to our learning curve is a gratifying realization. Each person is a gift, clearly. And we are gifts in the lives of others too.

While it is true that everyone comes forth with a lesson for us, some lessons will tax our patience more than others. A few will be simple reminders. On occasion, we will choose to wander away from a lesson, for now. We know it will return at a later time. In total, our lives are purposeful. And we come together with others for both learning and teaching when we have a shared purpose, one we agreed to undertake together in a far earlier time, a time now long forgotten.

I am comforted so often by recalling that no one is unbidden on my journey. No one. Being afraid of who or what might come next is no longer even a consideration. How I wish I had understood this as a child. Even in early adulthood I often felt afraid. I felt that others understood things that had simply slipped by me. I seemed always on edge, expecting something dire to happen. And unfortunately, we can and often do draw to us things that seem to fit our fears. Our egos love to throw us off balance and do so as often as possible.

There are no accidents. Our journey through life has been scripted, and with our help.

Let's never forget that there is another voice vying to get our attention at every moment. Remembering this quiets the nerves in those times of confusion. Simply know that we are always in the right place at the right time. There are no accidents. Our journey through life has been scripted, and with our help. The work we are here to do we have agreed to do. The lessons we are learning we have agreed to learn. The men and women we are meeting we agreed to meet. Always, all is well.

I fully embrace everything I am sharing in these essays. And yet, there was a time I scoffed at nearly all that I share with you now. Surely I didn't agree to experience the abuse, sexual and emotional, that troubled me for so long. Why would I have agreed to a marriage that was so fraught with pain and sorrow? And did I really need to nearly lose my life to alcoholism? And yet to all these experiences and more, I said yes. Yes. That's a part I will play in the evolution of our lives, yours and mine. That each experience seemed unfamiliar and hardly expected should not surprise us, you and I. That we come to understand, in time, how lives unfold is the gift that awaits all of us.

The unfolding of our lives is like a beautiful composition. The conductor knows exactly what each note will be and which musician will perform it. The interplay between the many performers is well scripted; indeed, the entire piece is intentional, and the melody is sometimes joyful, sometimes not. However, the total composition is perfect, simply perfect.

One of the greatest gifts of growing old with the course is being blessed by the comfort that has come with knowing this is a classroom and my purpose here is to be an example of love, wholehearted love, wherever I am. I believe, too, in the butterfly effect. The coupling of love with the butterfly effect means that every time I greet another person with kindness, my action ripples forward, positively impacting the universe of seven billion people.

Likewise, every time I am unkind, unloving, or mean-spirited, I am spreading discontent throughout the universe. Our assignment is so simple, should we care to complete it: be kind. Most days I am willing. Are you?

❧

We can change our minds and change the world we see. And what we see is what we experience. The power is ours.

Chapter 14

We cannot change the world, but we can change our minds about the world.

I find this concept beautiful in its simplicity. But often, I try to change the world anyway. As well as a bunch of the people in it. Even though I know my longing to change others is futile, far too many minutes are given to that endeavor rather than embracing peace, unadulterated peace, which is always available to me. To you too.

The choice between being at peace and being agitated about circumstances and people we have no control over should be an easy one. It obviously isn't. It doesn't take more than a glance at the Internet or a newsstand to see how very engaged millions of people become in situations that could and should have been left alone. That's the nature of being "victimized" by the never-silent ego.

Its work is never done. Until the ego has successfully engaged us in interfering in business that really isn't ours it doesn't feel fulfilled. And the irony is that when it does engage us, as it so often does, we can't be fulfilled.

Coming to believe that we cannot force change upon the world is the first step to freedom. Unfortunately, we seldom appreciate the freedom, at first. Instead, we feel cheated that we have no power to control the actions of those whom we travel among. We mistakenly assume, since we walk side by side, that our business should be shared, intermingled in fact. Living with that assumption has made our lives tumultuous at the very least. Wouldn't moments of quiet peace be a welcome change?

There are men and women all around us who serve as great examples of the peaceful life. You no doubt have noticed them. You meet them at work or the grocery store, even the gym too. In the long line of traffic that ensnared us on our way home from work, many were moving forward in the traffic unruffled by the incessant stop and go. How do they do it?

Changing one's mind is the one change we all have the power to undertake.

They have no magic powers, but what they do have is control over their own thoughts, their own emotions, and their own actions. Changing one's mind is the one change we all have the power to undertake. What's holding us back? Little more than habit. We have years of practice trying to control the uncontrollable. Allowing others to be who they want to be is simply a seldom-tried activity. Making the decision to step away from the lives of others seems unnatural to most of us. Aren't they here, by our side, because of the good we can do for them?

What those peaceful ones in our midst know, which many of us have yet to figure out, is that not expending our energy on trying to change the world around us gives us so much more time and energy to accomplish the purpose for which we were born. Nary a one of us is purposeless. I am relieved by this—especially on those days I feel less focused. Knowing that I do have a purpose, and that each of you has a purpose too, is comforting. Very comforting.

Our purposes are sometimes intermingled, which might confuse us at first. But having an assignment that relies on two or more people still doesn't make us accountable for the part someone else is supposed to play. As we grow accustomed to making better choices and then reaping the benefits of those choices, we will grow more inclined to repeat what we are learning; and in the process, new habits will be grooved. And for every healthy habit that we demonstrate, others are influenced by the example.

The irony is obvious. We can't change or control others, but our better behavior is noted, sometimes imitated, and always considered. The world outside will, in fact, begin to change as we, one by one, change.

Changing our minds, in time, changes everything. Inner joy is a by-product.

Chapter 15

Anger is the all too common mask for fear.

This course principle offered me a lot of relief when I first encountered it. Fear felt a bit more manageable, far less dangerous and unpredictable, than anger—particularly others' anger.

I grew up amidst near-constant, verbalized anger, but I never knew that beneath it lay fear. Perhaps if I had known that, I'd have looked more acceptingly on my parents, my dad in particular. His anger was so often evident, and it erupted, irrationally, many times a day. There seldom needed to be a legitimate, initiating event for his anger to find expression.

Eventually I did find out what his fear was about, but for most of the first four decades of my life I simply cringed, felt sickened, or reacted to his anger, whether it was directed at me or not. And I sat in judgment, always.

He was particularly abusive toward my mom and my younger brother, most specifically shaming them for not doing something the way he would have done it. As they cowered, I felt compelled to stand up to him on their behalf. My reaction helped no one.

The turning point for my dad and me came in the context of an interview I did with him, specifically about the events of his life. I explained that I wanted to know him better. I had enrolled in a family of origin class and our primary assignment was to interview our elders to discover the patterns that most probably governed our lives. How surprised I was when my dad said that he had been afraid every day of his life, since childhood. He had never appeared afraid to me, and I had not yet been introduced to the concept that anger masks fear.

His parents had expected perfection from him, and his failures were met with derision and shame. He transferred all that he had been taught to our family. His behavior mirrored that of his parents. I simply had not known about his struggles. As he shared, my heart softened. Instantly. He never quit being angry. Never. But I no longer had to react or judge.

Learning, as I did, that anger covered up fear allowed me to see my dad and many of my companions in a new light. And I was able to feel genuine compassion where before I was full of judgment. The added benefit of coming to understand the real cause of anger was that I no longer had to withdraw from strangers who were uncomfortable to be around. Seeing fear in the eyes of others allowed me

to join with the hearts of people who simply needed acceptance and understanding.

Every person I meet is reflecting fear or love.
Every one of them.

I have had many years now of looking at the world
from a new perspective, and it has completely changed
my response to life. Being an expression of love in the
face of fear is a choice I can more easily make. Trying to
love angry people is far harder than loving folks who are
simply afraid. And every person I meet is reflecting fear
or love. Every one of them. Knowing this has changed
my life completely. And yet I still have to be reminded
occasionally. My eager ego is all too comfortable reacting to anger, in whatever form it has taken, in a like-
minded way. How glad I am that every minute offers a
new beginning.

Being a daily practitioner of love is a worthy purpose. And any day that I awake a bit troubled or off kilter,
I can right size myself in the blink of an eye by simply
remembering that loving others is my full and complete
purpose. And if the expression of love seems a stretch
because of the particular circumstances, being kind will
satisfy the assignment.

Anger is nothing more than fear. No matter who is
expressing it and regardless of the gravity of the moment.

Quiet kindness, love in a soft way, will change the tenor of the moment and the heart of the people present. Take my word for it.

Not having to be afraid of anyone's anger anymore is so freeing. And being willing to simply be an expression of love makes every situation soft. And so appealing.

Chapter 16

Would you rather be peaceful or be right?

What a conundrum. The obvious answer should be peaceful, but I have spent many anxious moments, years of them, in fact, insisting that I am right. And in the process, I've argued with anyone who may be listening that I am right too, of course.

I came by my need to be right "honestly," as some would say. In my family there was constant tension over who was right. My dad was the protagonist. He was terrified of ever being wrong. Seldom did anyone argue with him—except me, that is. I felt it was my duty to take a stand, representing the silent family members. I did no one any good. However, I made my need to be right habitual. I was my dad's best student.

I carried my need well into adulthood. When I first heard the question "Would you rather be peaceful or be right?" I had a ready answer. I had never consciously longed to feel peaceful. At that time, in fact, it seemed an odd choice. But being right was empowering. It energized me. Even when I was clearly wrong, acting as if I was right ignited something in me. What a sad declaration. An even sadder way to live.

I consider my introduction to *A Course in Miracles* one of the high points in my life. In fact, attaining a PhD is the only thing that outranks it. Little by little, every detail of my thinking began to change.

Perhaps not surprisingly, a book I wrote a few years ago focused on how we can change our minds. The book, *Change Your Mind and Your Life Will Follow*, was my attempt to help others realize how amenable our minds are to changing when the directions for doing so are simple and clear. Writing that book strengthened my commitment to living a less scattered life, a life that had always been in the midst of someone else's journey—actually, anyone else's journey, if truth be told.

What became abundantly clear to me the longer I studied *A Course in Miracles* was that inner peace, a primary goal for course students, would never become available to me as long as I tried to make the business of others my own. Deciding what was right for anyone else, or trying to, that is, was always the path to dis-ease and turmoil. More often than not my interactions with others began to look like the interactions that had prevailed in my family of origin. Peace was simply in very short supply.

I certainly don't think my rocky journey to this life that has finally been blessed by frequent, peaceful interludes is out of the ordinary. Few of us live among the truly peaceful; thus, the standard bearers we watch are, like us, seeking moments of peaceful respite too. Far more common are the communities that experience the near-constant throes of upheaval. We see them highlighted on the evening news and read about them on our phones, our computers, and every other device that serves up to the minute chaos for "our enjoyment."

The opportunity to see peace beckons
to us constantly, regardless of the
multitude of distractions.

The opportunity to see peace instead of this beckons to us constantly, regardless of the multitude of distractions. And on our more attentive, thoughtful days, we do choose peace over all the other responses we might consider. The good news is that we can make the choice that comforts us, inside and out. It's also the choice that benefits the rest of the human community too—and not just the neighboring community, but the *entire* human community.

What a glorious opportunity we have been given to make a difference that ultimately impacts men and women and children, worldwide. And just a thought ago, we were part of the problem.

My opportunities for making a
difference are as frequent as the
moments in this day that stand before
me. Please, God, help me choose wisely.

Chapter 17

Grasp fully this moment only and discover peace.

O ne at a time. Just one tiny moment at a time. That's all we need to know peace. That's all we have, in fact. One moment. One sacred moment at a time.

Living fully within the moment is a learned behavior for most of us. Perhaps monks and clerics from various religious practices have an easier time living in the powerful now because of the hours they spend in quiet prayer. But it's quite likely even they had to commit long hours to developing and then strengthening their devotion to prayer before they could turn off the world around them. They have no special faculties, after all. They are men and women, just like us. They simply are more rigorous, perhaps, in their adherence to prayer and silence.

Of course, their practice is not unique to them. We could commit to it too. Right now. But if we want to follow their lead and grasp each moment fully, there are certain steps we need to take. We must slow our minds, quiet them as completely as we can, barely taking note of each fleeting thought as we gently let it slip away. The key to appreciating *now* is letting the thoughts that distract us silently slip away primarily unnoticed, for certain unremembered, and definitely unneeded. Nothing more than this is necessary if we want to absorb the richness of the single, sacred moment that is calling to us.

The key to appreciating now *is letting the thoughts that distract us silently slip away primarily unnoticed, for certain unremembered, and definitely unneeded.*

What's the reward that awaits us when we rest within each moment as it pays its visit? It's a sense of well-being coupled with an inner peace that washes over us and all around us. In this moment we know that all is well. Within every moment all is well.

Few of us are in the company of people who choose quiet contemplation as a steady practice. Far more common are the folks who live in the fast lane, men and women who seem to fear that life is passing them by so they'd better rush to wherever they are going so they won't be left out in the cold. It's not easy to live even a slightly more contemplative life when we surround ourselves with friends who prefer the chaos of the ego. Indeed, its chaos beckons to us all.

It's fortunate that by making a simple decision we can turn away from the chaos just as quickly as we let ourselves be ensnared by it. Even though it's ever present doesn't mean that we have to be present to it. Ever. We choose what we give our attention to. And pulling our attention away from the chaos is the first step toward seeking the peace of the Holy Spirit that is always inherent in each moment that is moving, always, toward us. We can't escape the moments as they come. But we can be certain that we will appreciate them more if we let the Holy Spirit translate the moment for us.

What a blessing the course messages are. They continue to visit our minds even when we pay little heed. They don't shame us. They quietly wait for our attention. And when we continue to ignore the lessons, or forget them, they are repeated in a new way in case we've become ready to listen. As I mentioned a bit earlier, Jesus patiently reminds us in chapter eight, "If you want to be like me I will help you, knowing that we are alike. If you want to be different, I will wait until you change your mind." How healing are his words. We are never actually wrong, only slow in changing our minds.

Appreciating each moment, as it comes, is quite likely the biggest change any one of us will ever make. And it is the single change that rightsizes us in all matters. Nothing in our lives will remain as it was when we awake to living one sacred moment at a time. There is simply no joy like being absorbed by this moment only. And once we really connect to this phenomenon, life will no longer baffle us. Peace will be ours.

There is no mystery to living slowly and
deliberately. And there is no process that will
offer us greater rewards. May we breathe
in life a moment at a time, for this next five
minutes, and feel the change.

Chapter 18

We have access to two voices in our minds. Which one will we listen to?

Being aware that two voices are calling to us each moment of our lives is the first step in making the choice to listen calmly, slowly, and carefully rather than acting rashly. The first voice we generally hear is governed by the ego. It's loud, demanding, and it seldom says anything kind or helpful. Its motivation isn't loving. It always comes from a place of fear and wants to push us to behave in ways that reflect that fear. However, pausing long enough to hear the far quieter voice of the Holy Spirit will help us be an example of love. In all circumstances, in every encounter, within each moment, we can be loving.

The ego has had us in its grip for much of our lives. Let's not be ashamed of that. What happened in the past is done. But we can choose to turn our attention to the other voice now and make a fresh start. It's a decision.

Nothing more. Our impact on the world around us will be noted. Instantly. And the voice that got our attention will be obvious.

Some might think it's unfortunate that two voices vie for our attention every minute. I say, on the contrary. It empowers us to listen intently before making the choice that defines our behavior. We can celebrate the fact that nothing external to us needs to influence our choices. What we decide to say and do in response to every opportunity for action that comes our way is inviolate. We decide. We choose. We act. We are responsible.

*What we decide to say and do in response
to every opportunity for action that comes
our way is inviolate. We decide. We choose.
We act. We are responsible.*

I was genuinely relieved when the concept of the two voices was explained to me. That was decades ago, of course, but I still remember the palpable relief I felt. At long last there was an explanation for the confusion I so often felt. I knew I was being pulled in different directions, but I didn't understand that two distinct voices were calling out to me. In my youth I wasn't much interested in pausing, giving the quieter voice time to be heard. I was comfortable being brash. And harsh. I was even more comfortable denying that there might have been another response I could have made.

With maturity comes myriad blessings, many of them unexpected, and a few, completely surprising. We have changed, some of us dramatically so. And for those who haven't discovered much change yet, it is on the way. Peace, as a life choice, is available to us. All that's required for us to enjoy near-constant peace is being willing to surrender our attention to the quieter, kinder voice. It won't depart, ever. Our not choosing it all that often in our youth doesn't chase it away. It's patient. It will wait until we decide to listen. What a relief. Nothing we can do will make it disappear.

Perhaps you are wondering what has given birth to the two voices. The course explanation is comforting because it reveals how this classroom we share is organized. The quiet voice, the one attributed to the Holy Spirit, was given to us by God when we dared to deny our oneness, dared to deny that we were still at home in Heaven.

And why did we make that claim in the first place? Because we wanted to take charge of our lives, separate from the loving God who was our source of strength. Because we have free will, we were allowed to separate ourselves from the whole—but not without a thread that would lead us back. That thread is the kinder, quieter voice that God called the Holy Spirit. It has one job. And we occasionally allow it to be manifest in us. In time, it will be the sole voice we will listen to. In time.

Choosing the quieter voice as my guide
offers me freedom; freedom from anxiety,
freedom from conflict, freedom from the
insanity of my choices in the past. Every day
can be peaceful now. The choice is mine.

Chapter 19

The world we see is a witness to our state of mind.

How profound is the truth encompassed in these twelve ordinary words. How profound, indeed. According to *A Course in Miracles*, there is nothing "out there" at all. Nothing. No real brick-and-mortar world. Our own ego mind projects whatever we see, down to the tiniest details. And the part of our mind that we are aligned with in any one moment determines the view.

I love the simplicity of the course. There is " truth" and there is illusion. There is love and there is fear. Each is inviolate, uncompromising. Each seeks our acceptance.

The course principles adamantly proclaim that we see *only* what we want to see—not an easy concept to swallow. We hear *only* what we want to hear. Can this really be true? And finally, we experience *only* what we have planned on experiencing. There are no actual surprises in one's life. It flows as ordered by us and our learning partners in a far earlier, long-forgotten time. We can trust, with certainty, that no experience is superfluous; each one is divine and fits snuggly into the evolution of our being.

We have been prepared, in every instance, for whatever transpires.

We are observers as well as actors in the drama that unfolds as our lives. We can interpret this as exciting if we choose to embrace the many details that are uniquely our own. We have been prepared, in every instance, for whatever transpires. Even when the lesson seems harsh, perhaps cruel, we have agreed to it. We know it's part of our learning curve, a learning curve that informs and strengthens us as well as the many others who walk with us as friends, family, and strangers, each one a teacher or a student, depending on the specific circumstance.

I didn't like this particular truth when I was introduced to it many years ago. Being responsible for how every situation in my life paid its visit seemed unfair. Blaming others for how I felt had become so comfortable. I couldn't fathom how accepting responsibility for every experience in my life was a good thing and a growth opportunity at the perfect time too. I simply didn't embrace the idea that *there are no accidents* very quickly. Had I trusted this sooner, much of the pain of my life could have been avoided. My resistance made life harder than it was meant to be.

Our resistance to anything strengthens it, much like whatever we focus on grows in proportion to the attention we give it. The point is this: we exacerbate whatever the circumstance is. Our attention never softens the experience. Rather, it mimics the fertilizer we give to our flowers and bushes. A tough situation becomes tougher. However, letting go of our judgment, giving up the need to analyze and confront, allows the passing of experiences that were never designed to hurt us.

Taking responsibility for all that we witness, for how we see and feel and interact with the people and the circumstances in our lives, shouldn't overwhelm us. On the contrary, being completely responsible can free us from the victim role that kept us feeling small and insignificant. Acknowledging that we are in charge, that we are the actors rather than the reactors in our lives, allows us to define not only who we are in this moment but strengthens our resolve to keep defining ourselves in every tomorrow that is assigned to us.

Our journeys are specific, unique, intentional, and destined to be purpose-filled and necessary to the lives of those we travel among. We can take a deep breath and trust that all is well. We are in the right place at the right time. We need not be ruled by fear.

Wherever we go today has been divinely decided.
Whatever we learn or teach today is perfect too.
As has been suggested in other essays, nothing
about our lives is accidental. Nothing. Let's pause
and breathe easily. All is well.

Chapter 20

To shift your state of mind, make the choice to be loving regardless of the situation.

What a pleasant realization that we, and we alone, control what's in our minds. No one else can affect us without our willingness to let them take charge. And what's even better is this: *you can change your mind and your life will follow.* You are the sole proprietor of your state of mind. But of your mind only!

How we wish, far too often, that we had the kind of control over others' minds that we have over our own. We do want others to show up in our drama the way we have scripted them. That's human nature, perhaps. And while that may be true, it's also a relief to be free of the stress of being in charge of others' minds. It's quite enough to be saddled with our own mind. Period.

The positive aspect of this truth is that we can be as happy, as joyful, and as peaceful as we want to be by shifting the perspective we have at any one moment. And although we can never change how anyone else chooses to think and act, we are often surprised by how accommodating others become when we change our minds and treat them lovingly, regardless of the experience we have been sharing. Even though we can actually never control others' actions, when we change our own behavior, those we are traveling among often seem to change in positive ways.

Even though we can actually never control others' actions, when we change our own behavior, those we are traveling among often seem to change in positive ways.

Let's consider a few of the situations in which we might choose to be loving. Perhaps a neighbor begins to pry into our affairs and we are distressed by their actions. It's certainly not surprising that this may upset us; however, when others are not being kind, it's generally because they are afraid. And people who are filled with fear often behave in ways that seem unkind to others. Giving the neighbor the benefit of the doubt goes a long way in fostering the kind of good relations that can eventually change a whole community.

I certainly have been guilty of snarling at others when I was feeling afraid; and I can't expect others to behave any differently. But what I also know is that when others were kind in spite of my behavior I felt an inner shift. And it was a shift that resulted directly from the actions of others. What is obviously true is that even though we cannot directly control what anyone else chooses to think or do, we can sometimes influence the behavior of others through our own willingness to be kind and generous in our actions.

One of the situations that I find most difficult is when I'm in conversation with my spouse or a good friend and we have a difference of opinion. Instead of simply accepting that our opinions differ and moving on, one of us in the exchange doesn't move on. Sometimes I am guilty of this. Sometimes my spouse or friend is. Not always being in agreement is perfectly fine; in fact, it makes for good discussions as long as all opinions are allowed as well as respected.

Anytime the disagreement gets ugly or tense is a perfect opportunity to choose kindness over any response that might call to us. We need never be on the same page in our opinions, but we always need to behave with respect. And making the decision, once and for all, to be kind regardless of what our egos might be pushing us to do or say will always be the best decision. Being the one who influences others to become their better self by always being an example of our better self simplifies life. Ours and everyone else's too.

Making the choice to be kind or loving might be considered a selfish choice. Why? Because it benefits the giver as well as the receiver. That matters not at all. Being kind and loving in every situation that calls to you will always give you a sense of well-being. Nothing around us stays the same when we make the choice to be kind. We change and the circumstances change along with us.

Nothing is as easy as deciding to make
a tiny shift in our perception, and that
tiny act rewards us in very big ways.

Chapter 21

Every word uttered is coming from a place of love or a place of fear.

This is a powerful idea. And it's one that has truly simplified my life, when I remember it. Unfortunately, I spent decades developing an old habit of trying to discern why the people on my path did what they did, or said what they said. Old habits are hard to change.

I was obsessed with trying to figure out what others were thinking and why so I could orchestrate my thoughts and actions to blend with theirs. I wanted to be valued and assumed that the way to get what I sought was through being like-minded. My need for acceptance by everyone controlled me completely.

I have come a really long way since then. Being a student of the course has benefitted me as well as my family and friends for many years now. I no longer live in constant anxiety about their behavior, trying to discern what their actions mean and then wondering if the situation requires something from me. Being able to simply walk away from situations that used to engage me in unproductive and unnecessary ways has freed me to do only what I need to do.

*Being able to simply walk away from
situations that used to engage me in
unproductive and unnecessary ways has
freed me to do only what I need to do.*

Accepting that every expression uttered by anyone is telling their story, and nothing more than that, is so obvious. Why did it take me so long to understand a truth so simple? If others' words or deeds aren't kind and loving, they are afraid. And I am not at fault. Plain and simple.

When I know someone is filled with fear, I am filled with an inner willingness to be kind, regardless of what they said or did. My heart is immediately touched by the hurt that's registered in their words. We make our lives so much more difficult than they need to be. Making the decision to be kind to everyone, everywhere, in every situation, could be made one time only. And all the universe would feel a shift if that did occur. All the universe.

We add to or subtract from the joy experienced by everyone each time we utter a word. Accepting responsibility for how we are impacting the world at large isn't always to one's liking. However, when we look at the opportunity each encounter gives us, an opportunity that can truly make a positive difference in the lives of so many others, it's with humble pride that we can say, "Yes, I'll do my part."

Doing one's part toward making the universe a more loving place for everyone is such a worthy purpose and it asks so little of us. Just consider your thoughts and words and actions before addressing any situation and your presence will benefit everyone.

Chapter 22

The Holy Spirit has every answer we need.

What a blessing to know that we will never be forgotten; that at any moment, every answer we seek is never more than a brief pause away. All that is asked of us is that we be willing to pause. It's in the pause that we receive the words we need to hear or the nudge to follow one path or another. It's in the pause that we are assured of the love and the direction that everyone on our path needs too.

We are the way-showers. We have been selected to share the message of love that this world so desperately needs. How fortunate that the Holy Spirit is forever available to remind us of the only thoughts we will ever need to hold, the only words we will ever need to share, the only actions we will ever need to make. Our only assignment, as we embark on this journey as way-shower, is to be attentive to the right voice in our minds, the quieter voice. It will not be the first one we hear, so beware.

We are the way-showers. We have been selected to share the message of love that this world so desperately needs.

I have shared similar ideas before, but I have learned that helpful ideas can't be repeated too many times. As the course tells us, "I am here only to be truly helpful . . ." A simple admonition. Very simple. Unfortunately, the ego has a way of making us forget what our true purpose is. The ego prefers that we live in fear that then prompts us to say and think things that aren't helpful to anyone—not to us as the thinker, and certainly not to those who hear our words or experience our actions.

Never having to wonder what we need to do or say next makes our lives so simple, so quiet, so serene. In years past, when we were being controlled by the ego, our lives felt frantic. They were frantic, in fact. The ego never wants us to be peace-filled. It loses control over us when we aren't agitated. We can live a non-agitated life, however. A completely peaceful life. We need make only one simple decision: Seek the counsel of the Holy Spirit. Always.

Some days it seems easy to forget how simple life can be. Perhaps we get pulled off course because of a stressful phone call or an angry family member. Maybe a work colleague is trying to make us responsible for an error she made. Or maybe nothing at all really happened. We simply wake up feeling alone, alienated from our loved ones and from God. That's the nature of life at times. Where does the feeling of separation come from? It's not likely we will ever know for sure; but as soon as we recognize the symptoms, we can restart our day. We can quickly acknowledge the quieter inner voice that is never absent and begin to be the helper we were sent here to be.

Our job description is actually quite simple, isn't it? Pause, become still, and listen. Only then should we become willing to share the love that we hear expressed. Let's remember, for a moment, that every expression uttered by anyone is emerging from a place of fear or love. When we hear anything that isn't kind, we can actually be grateful because we know it's the opportunity God has chosen for us to experience so that we can be an extension of love.

Coming to believe, as I do, that I never meet anyone accidentally in this classroom, that I never experience anything that's not divinely chosen for me here, has completely changed the tenor of my life. I cannot help but be in the perfect place at every moment. I cannot help but hear the voice of the Holy Spirit if I willingly pause and listen. And I can't avoid being the way-shower of love when I remember how perfectly my life has unfolded.

There are no accidents. You are where you need to be at this exact moment. Listen to the small inner voice and know love.

Chapter 23

Every encounter is a holy encounter.

This thought sends angel shivers through my body. How quietly perfect each meeting is that we experience, every meeting long ago selected for this place and time. How I wish I would never forget this; but alas, I do, and then I have to address my uncertainties all over again. How human I am. And you?

Being reminded, as I am reminding both you and me right now, that everyone who crosses one's path is divinely chosen, offers me a big sigh of relief. The visitors are not showing up uninvited and by chance. I have sent for each person. Likewise, you have too. We simply don't remember the selections we made, the "contracts" we signed, so long ago, in a far-off time and place, contracts we were very willing to sign, according to Caroline Myss, a spiritual intuitive. Her discussion of this process, if unfamiliar to you, is beautifully explained in her book *Sacred Contracts*.

I feel certain of the truth of this. So let's relax and enjoy whatever lesson accompanies each encounter. It may be one about love, or possibly fear. It may startle us at first until we remember that each lesson is wearing our name. I am reminded, too, that I don't have to relish each lesson when it first appears. I can even refuse to be informed by it. It matters not when I learn the lessons that are perfect for me. Each one of them will pay another visit if I have turned away. The same is quite true for you.

We are not growing and learning haphazardly. There is a rhythm and a design that each encounter, every experience, is helping us weave.

Taking a few minutes every day to be grateful for all the lessons that have blessed our lives so far helps us to be ready for each of the subsequent ones. Reflection helps us see the pattern that is developing in our lives. We are not growing and learning haphazardly. There is a rhythm and a design that each encounter, every experience, is helping us weave, just like threads in a tapestry. And the final picture will fill us with awe.

I often marvel at how perfectly our lives unfold. It continues to mystify me why my soul selected each encounter that I have experienced. And yet, each one of them has added a touch of brilliance to the tapestry that is me. My picture is still coming into focus, so I know that I have many more encounters until it's time to call it a day.

Isn't it glorious that we need not worry over the end, neither when it comes nor how? By divine appointment the final experience has been charted. My showing up was determined long ago. And until then, one step, one lesson, one encounter at a time. All I need to do is be patient and remember that the best response to any experience wearing my name is an expression of love in one form or another.

Holy encounters, one and all. Wherever we are, they are too. And this will never change. How can we doubt the truth of our being? It is sacred. And perfect. And absolute.

We are exactly where we need to be.
We are meeting whom we need to meet.
We are learning what we need to learn.
Thank you, God. Amen.

Chapter 24

Forgiveness is our primary assignment in this life, and the key to our happiness.

I think we actually have a number of assignments in this life. One is to be kind, even to our enemies. Another is to be loving. Accepting everyone we meet as a necessary and specifically chosen learning partner is a third assignment, and one that often baffles us. However, according to *A Course in Miracles*, our primary purpose, or assignment, in this life is to be forgiving—in particular, to be forgiving of ourselves for our judgments of others.

Judging others is second nature to many of us. We observed it in our families while growing up and became good imitators. We see it in our friends and coworkers. Judgment is even evident in the strangers we travel among. For certain, groups of people are quick to judge other groups. Neighborhoods do it. So do countries. Opportunities to forgive abound.

It's so easy to sit in judgment of someone else, and it happens most often when we feel like we aren't measuring up. It's been my experience that I'm more prone to being judgmental when I am feeling afraid or insecure in the setting I'm in. My judgments indicate that I have some work to do, work that entails immediately moving closer or listening more intently to the voice of the Holy Spirit.

My demeanor toward others always indicates which of the two voices in my mind I have been honoring.

My demeanor toward others always indicates which of the two voices in my mind I have been honoring. When I am being kind and loving, the Holy Spirit has been heard. If I am passing judgment, my ego has taken center stage. All too often it takes center stage. And whenever it does, it results in a sense of separation from all the others who travel beside me. And the alienation that follows gives rise to more judgment. Mistakenly, the ego assumes that judging others is the pathway to feeling secure, to feeling "more than." On the contrary, it's the surest way to greater feelings of loss and uncertainty. I know this all too well.

How very normal of us to feel insecure and uncertain on occasion. And yet, we are always safe and completely secure. That's because we are always in the comforting arms of God. Always. Whether we feel those arms around us or not matters little. They are there, nonetheless. They will always be there, whether we acknowledge them or not. I am so grateful that this is true. And even though I continue to judge and feel separate from others at times, I am not separate ever, nor am I being judged by God. Never ever. How can life offer us more than that?

Indeed, life can't offer more than that. God's presence is absolute. God's presence will always comfort us if we choose to be comforted. God's presence is forever. If you or I feel ill at ease, it's not because God left our side. Not ever can that be the case. Being reminded of this truth helps me. *At this very moment it helps me.* Some days— today, in fact—I am simply inclined to forget the truth of God's presence. And on these days I easily slip into fear, followed by judgment, and then I once again have to forgive myself for my forgetfulness. It's no wonder that forgiveness is our primary assignment.

When in our ego state we all too easily complicate our lives. And then we complicate the lives of others too. We push outward the separation we feel within. And yet another experience of insecurity sets in. God didn't move. As usual, we did. The opportunity to fulfill our purpose falls upon us once again. Forgiveness. Forgiveness always of ourselves for our too-constant judgment of others. Forgiveness for that which we imagine others did, even though our projections are all that ever happened.

Let's remember, *the outside world reflects our inner world.*
Always. And forever.

Our opportunities to forgive
ourselves and others will be plentiful
today. Fulfilling that great purpose
calls to us daily. Will you answer?

Chapter 25

When one door closes, another opens. God has a better opportunity for us.

I was introduced to this idea more than forty years ago, even before I became a student of *A Course in Miracles*. And I well remember doubting the truth of it. A closed door had always felt like failure, and yet, my friend insisted, "No. God has a better plan for you." She promised. How could she know that?

Over the years, I have discovered how right she was. Many doors have closed as I have wandered through the halls of life. And each time one closed, initially I'd feel the fear that I had been forsaken. But long before the fear embedded itself securely into my psyche, I'd get a glimmering of the blessing that was waiting behind the door that was next to open. Every time, the lesson was good, although never anticipated.

What I have grown comfortable with is the certainty that my trajectory is up, always up. Even when a boulder slips onto my path, it's never been too large to step over or around. I expect that to always be true. Our journeys are never about failure, even when we stumble for a spell. Our journeys are always moving us closer to the people we are destined to be, and as we walk, we will meet the teachers we need to know. Without the lessons, we would not grow. We would not be prepared to teach those who seek us out. Without the lessons, we'd falter, perhaps even lose our way for a time.

And then another door would open and we'd find ourselves safe and secure and certain of our steps once again.

The truth of this principle is that doors will constantly beckon to us. And every door opens or closes as scheduled. Even when a closing door makes us uncomfortable or momentarily afraid, it happens on cue. Nothing in our lives happens at the wrong time, or with the wrong people. The timing of every experience is perfect, predetermined, and divine. We have invited each previous door to both open and close at a far earlier place and time, now long forgotten. We have always been the planner of the plan that wears our name.

We have always been the planner of the plan that wears our name.

Every day we get the opportunity to greet every person we meet as the teacher he or she is. In every instance, behind every door, stands the next life experience we have been made ready for. We need not be frightened or surprised or mystified. The plan is unfolding as scheduled. Your plan and mine too. There are no accidents in this universe we share. We cannot help but be at the right place at the right time. The course is adamant about this. We cannot not meet the perfect teachers that we have agreed to learn from. We cannot not teach the students who are drawn into our sacred space. The contract was made. And we said yes.

Hopefully this principle gives you the relief it now gives me. I used to fret over every circumstance, both before it made its visit and during the experience. I worried needlessly about a plan that I'd already agreed to. I was overwhelmed with dread that I couldn't handle that which I had agreed to handle. But I never faltered for more than a moment. As soon as I remembered, "I signed up for this," I moved forward with courage. You can too. You will. We've already said yes.

As we stand before the many corridors of life, wondering which is the right one to move toward, let's remember that we can't make a mistake. We will eventually arrive at our appointed destination with the willingness to learn what the next teacher has to offer. This has been agreed to already.

There is no reason to worry ever again. You and I are fulfilling the plan we signed up for. Not a single experience is superfluous. Not one.

Chapter 26

Don't let the past define the present.

This is such an obvious idea that when I first encountered it my reaction was, "Of course! That's not new information." And then I promptly fell back into my normal way of seeing life that was through the lens of the past. I did this so unconsciously that I honestly didn't see how powerful my attachment to the past had become over the years. Habits are very hard to distinguish and then admit to. Bad habits are even harder to acknowledge and then own. And relinquish? Extremely difficult—nearly impossible, in fact.

It's unfortunate that relying on the past to understand the present is such a natural response. Therefore, we have to be more than a little vigilant to refrain from doing this. Repeatedly. For years we observed others making this choice in our family of origin. And, as might be expected, that constant pattern affirmed that this pathway was the correct one, the single right one.

We experienced the blowback of this pattern of interpretation in the workplace too, no doubt. It's far more common, as well as easier, to wander through life relying on the past to guide us or explain whatever we don't understand about the present than to look with fresh, uncompromised eyes at every circumstance that grabs for our attention. Allowing the past to explain the present saves time. So we mistakenly think.

Making the decision to let the past *be past*, is the first necessary step we must take if we want to see the truth of our journey. And it's not an easy step. In fact, we have to summon up a lot of willingness to even consider believing that the past is done with us. Kaput! The past served us well when it was the present, and only then. Every experience has a very short life. Every experience lasts only a moment, in fact. *A single moment.* And not a moment more.

Making the decision to let the past be past, *is the first necessary step we must take if we want to see the truth of our journey.*

Can that always be true? Even when the experience is traumatic, like sexual, emotional, or physical abuse; or seemingly monumental, like death, a divorce, or getting fired from a job? In actuality, there is no time but the now. Ever. No experience is deserving of more than its moment. Its one tiny moment, regardless of the gravity of the experience. When its moment is over, it's over. It no longer has any relevance in regard to any other experience. What a profound awareness to claim and then eventually celebrate. But we must. We simply must.

Perhaps you are wondering why this particular concept is so important, why I am devoting an essay to this one idea. There is an explanation, as you might expect. But only one. According to *A Course in Miracles*, time has no relevance, no existence even, except here in this classroom. There was no time prior to our adventure into this classroom, an adventure that in truth, *never really happened*!

The ego, which created itself, invented time and then kept us tied to it as a way of controlling us. Indeed, it has done a very good job of controlling us. And the more we focus on a specific experience beyond *the only moment it can claim*, the greater the power we give it. Thus, the more likely we are to dredge it up as a way to interpret additional experiences, all of those experiences that really have no relationship to any additional event.

Even though no experience from one's past has any concrete relevance to a present experience (or one that might be wending its way to us at this very moment, each one being inviolate, of course), there is a thread in our tapestry that represents each experience we have ever had. And the design that is created by our many threads woven together reflects our very personal experiences, which are definitely unlike any other design.

Each tapestry, actually all seven billion tapestries, make a single picture, the picture of us. As one. The paradox is that even though each one of us is unique, we quite perfectly blend together and make one whole, one holy whole. This awareness, for most of us, is a major shift in our perception, a shift that is described as "the miracle" in *A Course in Miracles*. We are living in the shift. We are creating the shift. We are the shift! Hallelujah.

Your journey is unique, as is mine. And
every one of us is necessary or the picture
of the Holy One is incomplete. The part
we are playing in the panorama is not
accidental at all. Let's be grateful that our
part needs us, and only us.

Chapter 27

Everyone is a messenger.

S eeing every person who crosses our path as a messenger who has come to reveal the next part of our
story is a most intriguing idea, one that's seriously worthy
of our attention. I have said that there are no accidents
regarding the unfolding of our lives, no accidental meetings, no inconsequential experiences. Whatever's next on
our agenda is, without a doubt, headed toward us this
very instant. There is both excitement and anxious anticipation as we wait for its arrival.

Being grateful for whatever presents itself, whether
it is a person or an experience, is the most beneficial
response we can make in every circumstance wearing our
name. Even when we aren't honestly glad about greeting
the next visitor on our journey, acting as if we are serves
us well. Acting as if has the power to change the outcome
of an encounter or an experience in a very positive way. It

just might be the most important tool you consider using today. And if you do apply it, after observing its impact on your experience you will quite willingly apply it again and again in the future.

The evolution of our lives isn't really as mysterious as we might have first expected. They make sense. Every aspect, each experience and encounter, has been pre-planned. We are where we need to be. We have met or will meet who we need to. We have been called to do certain work, and when we feel confused about a situation, which is certainly quite normal and to be expected, we must be patient and allow the guidance that is needed the necessary time to surface. It's on the way. Now.

When we review how our lives have unfolded up to this point, we can so easily see the sense of them. We can enumerate for ourselves and others the primary lessons we obviously agreed to learn. We can quite peacefully conclude that nothing that happened was beyond our capability to handle, nothing was meant to frighten us or steer us down dark alleys with no avenue of escape. Everything wore our name. This we can recognize completely and with ease. We were promised we'd never be given more than we and God together could handle.

Have we greeted each messenger in a loving and accepting way? It's not unusual nor should we be ashamed to say no. But knowing, as we now do, that everyone working their way to our side was invited to make the journey can change how we greet them. We need not resist the inevitable. But if we do, the lesson itself will visit again, wearing a different package in the future. What we came into this life to learn will be learned. If not the first time it is presented, perhaps the second or third time. The number of times matters very little. It's the lesson itself that matters. And only that.

How many messengers have come your way? Categorizing them might be a valuable exercise. From some we learned patience. Others taught us tolerance. Humility, for many of us, was the most important lesson of all. Giving up anger, seeing it for what it really is (fear), quiets the noise in our heads. Being willing to be a simple expression of love in myriad forms is the most far-reaching of all the lessons, and it's one that every person alive will be introduced to by at least one wandering soul. And love, for certain, brings greater benefit to the universe we are sharing with billions of other souls than any other lesson. Love dissolves fear. Love elevates hope. Love destroys resistance. Love inspires more love.

Since we are all messengers to one another, and since we are all necessary in the scheme of life, let's double up our efforts to be messengers of love wherever we travel today.

Since we are all messengers to one another, and since we are all necessary in the scheme of life, let's double up our efforts to be messengers of love wherever we travel

today. There is nothing better that we could do to benefit the universe we inhabit than to be peddlers of love.
And since, according to the course, there are really only
two expressions ever made—love and fear—let's choose
wisely which one we will shower on all those who are
within range of our messages today.

Being an example of love is most satisfying,
not only to others on our path but to
ourselves too. Being loving implies being kind,
and that simply feels good, from the tips of
our toes to the tops of our heads. I promise.
Prove me wrong, if you can.

Chapter 28

Being gentle is our pathway to peace.
When the journey began, most of us
had no idea what was in store for us.

To be gentle is a decision that can be made and remade as many times as might be necessary during one's waking hours. Possibly there are some people who needed to make this decision only once, for all time, but I have yet to meet them. Most of the spiritually driven individuals who have crossed my path appear to have made a commitment to the practice of gentleness within their ordinary encounters.

That certainly doesn't disqualify them from being considered "really good people." On the contrary, it simply means they are regular folks, quite like all the people they travel among. Indeed, very much like you and me. And making the *choice* to be gentle is usually necessary rather than automatic. Perhaps one day it will be automatic, a habit that most of us would like to acquire.

The decision to be gentle encourages our own inner peace, whether others are present to experience it or not. Our payoff is that *we are changed*. Regardless. As a matter of fact, that's the only payoff we can ever be certain of. In time we will realize that's actually enough. How we treat others defines who we are. It changes who we are in the moment too. We become the men and women we admire every time we make the choice to treat others gently, kindly, lovingly, the way we'd like to be treated too.

How we treat others defines who we are.

If this isn't one of your daily practices, perhaps you should consider making it one. Everyone deserves to be at peace. Everyone. Doing our part to encourage peace offers great benefit to the world we share with all others.

Try an experiment, a really simple one. Use a gentle voice all day long. With everyone. Why? Because your gentle nature, your soft voice, will please all the people on your path. And you will be transformed in the process. The only person we can ever change, for sure, is ourselves. And for that, we are actually pretty lucky. If it were up to us to be in charge of all the others on our path, we'd never be at peace. Never.

It's really not difficult to make the choice to live peacefully. In fact, living free of agitation is far easier than always being in turmoil. We have been around agitated people enough to experience the discomfort it causes them. We can see their anxiety. We can feel their fear. There is nothing attractive about how they are living. Choosing a peaceful path is so much more appealing.

The more often we make the choice to be gentle in all our responses, the easier our lives will be. And the easier our loved ones' lives will be too. While it's true that we can't control other people, we can influence them by how we behave in their presence. Every time we set a peaceful example, for one person or a group of friends or even a crowd of strangers, we will have made the kind of difference that really matters in this community of people who serve as our teachers and our students.

A Course in Miracles is truly a simple pathway for living in this world. However, the ego works hard trying to keep us from living peacefully. Its voice calls to us constantly, and that's because its very survival depends on being in charge of our thinking and our actions every minute.

Even though we have become aware that we have two voices in our minds, the ego speaks first and it speaks loudest. And it is always wrong. We have to truly want to hear the quieter voice calling for peace that comes from the Holy Spirit. The problem each one of us is faced with, unfortunately, is an ego that doesn't want us to be at peace, now or ever; an ego that hopes to create conflict so that it survives.

We need not give in to the ego, ever. The decision belongs to each one of us. I have decided I want to enjoy the quiet fruits of peace in these years that remain. Why don't you choose peace too? Adding your voice to mine is how we change the world we share with others. Nothing is stopping us.

Peace belongs to me. It belongs
to you too. We simply have to step
forward, quietly, and claim it.

Chapter 29

Acceptance is the doorway to discovering peace.

Ihave never awakened to the thought, "Wow. I feel totally accepting today." I have never even considered this exact thought before, in fact. Does this mean I'll never know peace? On the contrary. Peace is a state of being that we quietly, almost unknowingly, choose. It's not a state of doing. It simply washes over us, generally because we have come to realize that in this moment, *we need do nothing*. All is in its right place. All is perfect, as is, and needs no interference from us.

I love this quiet line, (*I need do nothing*) that's tucked away in the course text. It invites me to relax. To truly do nothing but remember that all is well. I can do nothing that will make *this present moment* even a tiny bit better.

Peace is always our gift when we simply stop. Breathe. And then breathe again. Sitting in this tiny moment of peace, content, alive in the knowingness that all is and always has been fine, just as is, pleases me. I am comforted, and yet I chase it away with my fearful thoughts. On the way to many occasions, I chase peace away. Fortunately, it doesn't really leave the premises. It waits close by, aware that I will be seeking that state of mind very soon, once again, perhaps in the very next moment.

I have had to accept my inability to live in this state of peace except intermittently. And it makes me sad. I'm thinking this struggle is normal, but I am also thinking that resting in the peaceful moments can't be all that hard. It's simply a state of mind. A chosen state of mind. The problem is that my choice is fleeting, intermittent, not constant. That's how life is for some of us.

Deciding to accept the experiences that visit us daily makes living so much easier.

Deciding to accept the experiences that visit us daily makes living so much easier. Those people and events that come calling are actually doing exactly what we have prearranged, before we awoke, here, in this place we all mistakenly call home. Unfortunately, we forgot the contract we made; thus, our egos often push us to resist whatever lesson is wearing our name in this moment. And peace eludes us.

The experience, whatever it is, is perfectly timed for right now, right here, with him or her. To decide to go with the flow and walk willingly into the experience would change everything about our journey, in an instant. Doesn't that appeal to you, at least in a tiny way? It would change every moment of the rest of your life, for the better, if you decided to gratefully accept that which you *agreed to experience* quite willingly at a time long ago.

Perhaps it's due to aging, but I have begun to think of *acceptance* as a soft word, an inviting word, a word that's like a quiet companionship. Even the sound of the word is nonthreatening. To me, acceptance says, "Let's just rest a while. Do nothing. Shall we?" And I willingly assent. Thinking of acceptance as a kind reprieve invites an inner smile, from me at least.

Choosing to believe that acceptance of any situation will lead to the quiet joy of peacefulness definitely makes the decision to accept life on life's terms easier. I want an easier, softer life. I have paid my dues. You have too. Making the decision to sit quietly amidst the many experiences I have yet to enjoy, *but did order*, fills me with peaceful anticipation. Nothing that is coming my way— nothing—is actually unexpected. I need not fret. Over nothing is there reason to fret.

❦

Our example will serve to show others what
peace looks like, what peace feels like. And
finally, how to make it one's own. Are you up
to the test? Join me.

Chapter 30

A miracle is a simple shift in perception. Nothing more.

One of the most helpful tools I have received from *A Course in Miracles* is the suggestion to seek the Holy Spirit's help by asking this tiny question: "Please help me see this differently." The very first time I sought His help, I received instant relief from my incessant drive to control whatever had nabbed my attention.

Even though I understood early on that "the miracle," as referred to by the course, was simply a shift in perception, I didn't immediately adopt this suggestion in my daily life. For some reason, I failed to grasp that if I utilized the Holy Spirit's help to see whatever was troubling me differently my life would become peaceful. And it would remain so every time I let the Holy Spirit guide me. What a failing that was.

When I seriously requested His help, I was utterly amazed by how quickly and how quietly my life changed because my perspective changed. What had been consuming my mind and controlling my actions, regardless of how large or small the irritant, simply seemed to dissolve. To melt away. Almost instantly, my heart felt lighter. And just as quickly, my mind cleared. Not more than a minute passed before I felt an inner shift that softened me, completely, and then bolstered my desire to express this feeling of love to all the people who were sharing my path.

Since that moment in time, I have tried to hang on to this tool. To make it a "daily driver," so to speak. Believing in the constant presence of the Holy Spirit offers such comfort. Whenever I want my life to change, my feelings to relax, my grasp on others to lighten, a simple request to the Holy Spirit comes to my aid immediately. What more could one ever want?

Whenever I want my life to change, my feelings to relax, my grasp on others to lighten, a simple request to the Holy Spirit comes to my aid immediately.

To never again be stuck in our old behavior and controlled by our earlier mind-set is so refreshing. So relieving. Seeking the help of the Holy Spirit, who is a mere thought away, has made us genuine change agents, serving all the men and women who are intentionally sharing our journey. What a powerful realization that is. I have met no one accidentally. I have had no experience that wasn't chosen by and for me. Whatever is left for me to experience in this life is already on its way to me, and if I'm troubled at all, I have the perfect solution. Ask the Holy Spirit to help me see the situation or the person differently. And the journey will become smooth.

There is no one reading this book who hasn't sought more peace in their life at some time. Conflict with others simply doesn't feel good. And yet we encounter those people who seem to seek conflict on a regular basis. What I have come to believe is that the only way we can truly appreciate peace is to be able to compare how it feels with its opposite. I don't think conflict visits us to ensnare us but rather to give us an opportunity to demonstrate another way to experience life. We are the teachers as well as the students on this journey. Demonstrating peace definitely puts us in the teacher capacity.

There are two voices in our minds. I have written about this many times. One belongs to the ego. The other one belongs to the Holy Spirit. Which one has your attention most often? Are you content with your life? If not, it's your responsibility to make a different choice. You and I are the miracle makers. And every time we choose again, we benefit so many. Is this on your agenda today?

Creating a miracle is no mystery. It's as close as the next thought we have. Do you want to see this or some situation differently? Now is your time to prove it.

Chapter 31

We decide the world we want
to see and then we create it.

This statement is both explicit, and strong. It definitely suggests no nonsense. We are in charge. There can be no argument about this. What I choose to see is my creation, and it's not likely to even remotely resemble what you choose to see. Unfortunately, our differences lead us into conflict; conflict within our families, our communities, and all too often between nations.

The need to be right is so important to everyone that disagreements easily reign everywhere. And when our egos have commandeered the creator's chair, an all too common occurrence, as evidenced by the demanding news cycle, conflict is assuredly rampant.

However, the Holy Spirit is just as available to us as the ego, and He can also be invited to create the world we see. When that has been our choice, we experience a very different world, a very different world indeed. We see and experience real joy; we know peace of mind, and we are able to express love ever so easily.

Why would anyone choose otherwise? It's hard to imagine, isn't it? And yet, the ego's voice is far louder in our minds, and *it always speaks first*. It will never be a party to a peaceful view of the world outside. Never ever.

Why do we so easily succumb to the demands of the ego? Just because it's louder than the Holy Spirit can't be the sole reason. It's my opinion that we succumb out of habit. We developed the habit as children, primarily because we lived among others who were obviously under the influence of their ego too, from the time we were born. Our friends are heavily influenced also, as are our coworkers. Wherever we look we see the work of egos.

Seldom does a loving story end up in our daily papers or on the evening news that highlights an experience that was clearly the result of some person allowing the Holy Spirit to guide their actions. Ego outbursts make the news; we are privy to many of them daily. And every one of them seems to trigger copycats. To most of us, "news" is equated with "bad news." What a sad realization this is.

Let's not lose hope, however. There is some good news, and it is that you and I share this classroom. Our primary assignment here is to remember what our egos have made us forget: *who we really are and where we actually live in spite of what we think is true*. Being told, as the course tells us many times, that we are Spirit, at one with God, still at home in Heaven, feels terribly unlikely because of the world we have allowed our egos to create.

Being bombarded by the mayhem *we and our egos have created* makes it very difficult to believe that what we see is an illusion we all subscribe to. Naturally we feel confused, doubtful, and very unsettled by the course teachings. How fortunate that many of us found study groups to guide us. As a result, we are coming to believe that this illusion is indeed a classroom, and one that is teaching us how to love and teach love too.

I can only speak from my experience, but I seem to have been born a fearful child and I lived fearfully for decades. Naturally, I created a fearful world because I listened solely to my ego. When I was finally convinced there was another voice I could hear, if I chose to be attentive to it, my world, and thus my life, began the shift that has brought me such joy in my advancing years.

"What one can do, all can do."

I want you to experience this joy too. That's the whole purpose for this book. I want others to know the peace I have begun to experience on a regular basis. And I'll tell you what others told me: "What one can do, all can do." Simply make it a practice of discarding the first voice you hear when you go within for guidance of any kind. You will be directed by the Holy Spirit. I promise. But

His voice will not be the first one you hear. Never will it be the first one. And His voice will not sound adamant and controlling. His voice will offer a loving solution to whatever you are asking.

This is a gentle path if we choose to listen to the gentle inner voice. And when that's our choice, we will help all those we encounter to know greater gentleness too.

Discovering who we really are is a
worthy adventure. Let's help one
another find the way beginning now.

Chapter 32

There is no struggle too big to relinquish.

I was raised in a home where there was no struggle too small to turn into World War III. My dad was our four-star general, and I all too willingly worked hard to follow in his footsteps. As might be expected, he insisted on being right regardless of what the disagreement was about. I always, absolutely always, took exception to his view no matter what topic was in question just because. . . . We knew our roles well and we performed this drama nearly every day to the benefit of no one.

How relieved I am, now that I am in the last quarter of my life, to be able to share with all of you the folly of my choices in my youth. It wasn't until my late thirties that I came to fully understand the pain of my dad's life, pain that was borne from fear and had been his companion since childhood. How sad it is that some of us live in the throes of fear for a lifetime. But his fear was disguised by his anger, anger that was in check at work but ran rampant nearly every day once he got home.

Learning, as I have, through my study of the course that every response made by anyone in any circumstance has been schooled by the ego or the Holy Spirit has not only enlightened me but also inspired hope that I can remember which inner voice gives me the most peace. For certain I will never be at peace if I follow the suggestions of the ego. My experiences throughout my life have been a testament of that.

I was accustomed to listening to the ego most of my first forty years. But once I got a taste of what listening to the Holy Spirit felt like, I yearned for the solitude of more peace. I wish I could say that choosing that quieter voice has firmly become my habit; it hasn't. But I have never forgotten what peace feels like, and on my good days I choose the softer voice as my guide and I experience peace that is always accompanied by joy and gratitude too.

How really insane it is that we so often listen to the noisy, mean-spirited ego, allowing it to decide for us what our next thought or action should be. And every time we succumb to this choice, we contribute to the unrest that permeates our entire world. What any one of us does is felt by every one of us everywhere. Perhaps that idea hasn't resonated with you yet, but it's true. So very true.

It's so easy to get off on the wrong foot upon arising. Whatever our first thought is often sets a pattern for all subsequent thoughts for the rest of the day. If you are like me, I used to assume the whole day would be miserable if I had an unpleasant first thought upon waking up, never even considering that it is possible to start the day over— at any time and as often as necessary. Understanding this is crucial if we really want to experience peace, instead of this, whatever "this" is.

I'm not proud of having to start over as often as I do; however, it's better than the alternative. There is no shame in beginning again. There is no shame, period, in any thing we do or don't do. That's one of the things we learn when we listen to the Holy Spirit. He will never shame us. On the other hand, the ego loves to shame us. And it repeatedly does so. The choice is ours. That's a truth that will never change.

We are never cajoled into turning to one voice over the other. But looking back over our interactions with others just from the last day or two will help us see which voice we've turned to more. How many struggles did we engage in? If we can comfortably acknowledge we were struggle-free most of the last few days, we are on our way to developing a habit that will assure us of peaceful living most of our waking hours. If that's not the case, we have work to do. Let's monitor all our choices from this moment on.

Walking away from a fight, big or small, is empowering. When I was younger, I simply couldn't pull myself away. One of the blessings of age is that what attracted me in my youth has lost its appeal. I learned in a twelve-step program that I don't have to attend every fight I'm invited to. What freedom that has given me. It certainly has contributed to a much quieter existence.

Making the choice to smile and walk away from an opportunity to go to battle will foster a change in your daily life that you can't quite imagine.

I can promise each one of you that making the choice to smile and walk away from an opportunity to go to battle will foster a change in your daily life that you can't quite imagine. Tarry not. Our seven billion–person universe needs the willingness of each one of us to choose the quieter pathway if we want to experience the shift to a more peaceful world that we all deserve.

Will you join me in choosing to walk away at least once today? Every new habit begins by doing something once. This is a wonderful "something" to do.

Chapter 33

Your mission is simple: live lovingly.

There is great beauty in such simplicity. There's no great mystery to the game of life. Walk softly. Carry no stick at all. Life isn't about winners and losers, even though the ego tries to convince us it is. And many of us have been trapped into playing *that* game for much of our lives. I certainly fall into that category. Probably many of you have spent years there too.

There is good news, however. The ego can only hold us hostage with our consent. Taking our power back is like no longer giving someone rent-free space in our minds. As I have alluded to many times, your life will be as filled with love and peace, joy and gratitude, kindness and helpfulness as you choose to make it. You are definitely in charge of your journey, and the opportunities that have and will present themselves have been ordered by you to practice your mission on.

*Your life will be as filled with love and peace,
joy and gratitude, kindness and helpfulness
as you choose to make it.*

The realization that you have asked for every experience that has knocked on your door is a helping of harsh
reality for some. I didn't like that information when I first
received it either. I resisted it vehemently, in fact. But
eventually I grew to embrace it. What it means to me now
is that I am more able to help others by sharing the difficult experiences I have survived and, in every instance,
grown from. They have served a very worthy purpose.
I'd have to say that's why all difficult experiences occur
for anyone. They are meant to inform many, not just the
people they happened to.

Perhaps some or even many of you won't willingly
accept what I am telling you here. That's your prerogative.
It's not necessary that you believe anything I say about the
experiences that have paid you a visit. However, believing that it benefits you and everyone else to be loving to
everyone on your path can still be practiced. And that's a
worthy mission—and our primary one.

Frankly, I love that our mission is simple. None of us
can be stumped by the question: "Is what I am about to say
or do what God would have me say or do?" If we can't give
a resounding yes, then we must refrain. It's really a very

good question, and it leads to a far more peaceful family, neighborhood, community, and universe when practiced.

"I can choose peace instead of this," one of my favorite shortcuts for simple living from the course workbook, is a marvelous and extremely simple way to monitor who we are bringing to the dinner table, the classroom, or the neighborhood gathering. Every time we make a loving gesture, we are contributing to a more peaceful world, one person at a time.

It is possible that living from a place of peace and love hasn't yet become as interesting and necessary to you as to as it has to me. Thus, this essay might not call to you. And that's fine. We don't all seek to know what we know at the same time. Our trajectory through this life is quite unique. Quite perfect for each one of us, as a matter of fact. You will learn what you came here to learn at the right time. Exactly the right time.

And I do think that as we age, we yearn for more quiet, more peace, for far less chaos and excitement than in our youth. It's also possible that I am further along the timeline of life than most of you. After all, I have entered the final quarter of my life. I have far fewer years to live than what I have already lived. And there's a nice feeling to that, actually. Perhaps I am satiated with all the wisdom I really need to live a fruitful life until my end.

I hope you don't interpret my words as maudlin. I'm certainly not feeling sad or dissatisfied. On the contrary, I'm feeling quite complete with who I have become, with what

I have learned and contributed to those I have encountered in person and through the books I have written.

In every one of them I felt led. Every word I have written has come to me from a power other than myself—a power far greater, as a matter of fact. This book, I can assure you, is coming to me in the very same way. And it pleases me to know that I have had a purpose and my higher power has been my constant companion.

You have your specific work just as I have had mine. But in both of our lives we do share the same mission: to live lovingly. We are one and the same in that pursuit, and that's a pleasing thought. Isn't it? Are you up to the task you have been sent here to perform? If you feel overwhelmed, at any time, remember that you have a helper. No task is too great for any one of us when we allow God to be part of our lives. As my mother-in-law told me so many decades ago, if I feel alone and lost, God didn't move: he has been waiting all along to walk us through our mission. The truth of our lives is so simple, so perfect, so unique, and so necessary in the tapestry that is busily weaving all of our lives into one glorious picture.

Living simply and lovingly is all that's
asked of us. Surely each one of us
can do that, one day at a time.

Chapter 34

We are here only to be truly helpful.

I am paraphrasing a prayer from the early part of *A Course in Miracles* that I find very comforting. Our "job" in this life is really quite simple: be helpful to every person who crosses our path. There are no exceptions, which makes our task exceedingly clear. Mother Teresa has been quoted as saying something very similar: "Be kind to everyone and start with the person standing next to you." These two sources satisfy me. Keeping it simple works.

If you walk toward me smiling, frowning, or even obviously angry, my assignment from God is unmistakable because "every loving thought is true. Everything else is an appeal for healing and help, regardless of the form it takes." In other words, anyone who isn't loving is appealing for our help, and the obvious help we can offer is to be loving, which in certain instances might best be expressed simply as a nod of acknowledgment. To repeat, there are no exceptions! Every expression is coming from a place of fear or love. Period.

I find it very helpful that those two emotions encompass every expression uttered or every action taken. It makes what is expected of me pretty easy to determine. If my companion is angry about something, it's my job to be understanding and helpful. Kind, at the very least.

> *"Every loving thought is true. Everything else is an appeal for healing and help, regardless of the form it takes."*

Many people who we meet will not be coming from a place of love. If I am among strangers who seem to be riled up about something, it's probably not in my best interests to interfere. Standing apart from the group, I can offer a prayer for their well-being and peace of mind. But getting involved in every scuffle or potential scuffle isn't the job you or I have been sent here to complete. My purpose, and yours too, is extremely simple: do no harm.

I heard a wonderful story about the Dalai Lama some years ago. I wasn't present at the event where he spoke, but I am grateful that I heard about it in detail because it sets the record straight about what is ours to do. He had been invited to be the guest speaker at a large fundraising event in California. The guests were excited to hear his message, as his audiences always are. After the dinner dishes were cleared away, and the master of ceremonies introduced him.

To thunderous applause, he approached the podium. When the room grew quiet, he said, "You are in this life to love one another." Following those few words, he stepped away from the podium and turned to leave the stage. The audience was stunned into silence, with the exception of a few who began whispering to those who were sitting close by. *How could this be?* they were obviously all wondering.

Much to the relief of the audience, the Dalai Lama returned to the podium. He very purposefully and quietly looked out over the crowd, moving his head from left to right. And then he cleared his throat and began speaking, once again, to all who had gathered for his message of enlightenment.

"And if you can't find it in your heart to love one another, just don't hurt one another." This time he not only left the podium, he left the stage too. What he had shared was truly the only message any one of us ever needs to hear. And if just a few of us heeded the message every day, before too long a critical mass of loving people would effectively change the universe.

Perhaps it hasn't ever registered for you the power that just a few can have when it comes to changing the mindsets of many. However, a critical mass can be reached by a mere 20 to 25 percent of the population, and that means the tipping point is closer than many of us had imagined. We have all heard the hundredth monkey story, and this tipping point I'm referring to follows the same pattern.

A very few can ultimately change very many. In fact, to paraphrase Margaret Mead again, it only takes one person to initiate a lasting change.

Our mission is simple. Be loving to everyone, everywhere. Greet all encounters with a loving heart and your purpose will be fulfilled.

Our time here is short. Our work here is special. Our opportunities are everywhere. Let's move forward together and make the difference that the universe is waiting for.

Chapter 35

Choosing the Holy Spirit as your constant companion promises a peaceful journey.

If only it were as easy as it sounds. And actually, there are many instances when the choice doesn't seem difficult to make. Particularly if the ego has been overly active, creating havoc where none need be. At those times I experience a real desire for quiet, for release from the chaos that so easily multiplies, for a helping of stillness. The beauty is that the Holy Spirit is not only willing to be my constant companion who can offer all of that, but He really desires to always be "on duty," maintaining that peaceful stillness, moment by moment.

It helps me so much to think of the Holy Spirit as an internal hovering angel who is always on call. When that's my image, and it frequently is, I feel safe, extremely comforted, regardless of where I am and who I am with. And the longer I have been committed to the course as my spiritual pathway, the better my life has been. I have become more peaceful, more joyous, and more willing to share the comfort I feel with others. I won't be an emotional wreck, creating problems for others who cross my path, as long as I adhere to the voice of the Holy Spirit more often than the voice of the incessantly noisy ego.

It's so obvious which voice others are listening to, isn't it? A person's demeanor clearly alerts all onlookers. Erratic, angry behavior signals danger, there's an ego at work. It's never our job to point out the folly of another's behavior, but we can model what honoring the Holy Spirit looks like. Any person modeling the thoughts of the Holy Spirit will be quiet in a loving way, and helpful to all in a clearly generous way.

Many of our daylight hours are spent with coworkers or acquaintances who may not choose to be on a spiritual path. It's not our task to point out ways their lives could be happier, even though we may have a strong desire to help them find what we have found. We can only really model for others another way to be or see. And when asked, freely share what we have learned about this illusion so many obviously think is real as opposed to the world you now so comfortably live in.

This is a classroom we share with billions of other individuals. Even though we are one, and even though we are *still at home in Heaven with God*, few of us trust, at all times, that this is the true state of our being. Your life and mine too will be so much easier when we can celebrate *our real journey, our real home, our real existence.*

Until we all understand the true state of this classroom, it's best if we wander quietly through each day simply serving as kind, loving examples to others of what being joined to the Holy Spirit looks like. Being a loving presence in the life of others is the kindest gift we can offer to friends and strangers alike. It really matters not. Our job is simple and the same in every encounter. If for a moment you doubt the simplicity of your assignment, remember that's what the ego wants you to feel. Deny it its control. Walk forward confidently and lovingly and *do the work you came here to do.*

Deny the ego its control. Walk forward confidently and lovingly and do the work you came here to do.

Some people might look at you with suspicion. That's probably because they doubt the availability as well as the reliability of a Holy Spirit who has been given to each of us by God so that we could, when our loving actions here are done, find our way home. And in the meantime, treat with kindness all the individuals, known and unknown, who have wandered your way with intent and with a lesson to teach. As I have said, there are no accidents. *None whatsoever.* And isn't that the good news? Are you not comforted by it?

I feel the need (actually, it's more a desire) to tell you all just how much I love traveling this particular path with you and with the Holy Spirit too. His presence has manifested a sweet world, one that has nurtured unexpected growth and successes. I have also learned innumerable lessons, not all of which pleased me at the time. But I have also been reminded that every single lesson was specific to me. Yours have been specific to you too. Again let me remind you, there have been no accidents.

Some reading this essay are in the first quarter of their life. Others, like me, are in the final quarter. It matters not. Anyone we need to meet still has time to find us. Any lesson we already agreed to teach will transpire just as soon as all the students have gathered. Isn't it calming to remember that there is not a single thing we need to worry over? Divine order is in charge. Our contracts with others will be fulfilled.

It thrills me (hopefully you too) that our lives
will be complete when the work we agreed to
do is done. And not before. It also thrills me
that all the people I have met came as called.
Our final encounters will be the sweetest of all.

Chapter 36

If the thought you are protecting wouldn't please God, exchange it for one that would.

This is one of those extremely handy reminders. It's simple, very adaptable, and takes only a fleeting moment to incorporate into your encounters with others. And when you do let this tool guide your interactions, you will discover peaceful relations with all the visitors on your radar. Let's always remember that whomever pays a visit hasn't just happened upon us. Their presence was expected—perhaps not remembered, but definitely part of the plan for our lives.

We are terribly lucky to have such simple yet ample guidelines for creating lives that can be considered helpful to others as well as beneficial to us. There is nothing complicated about monitoring our thoughts. It's as easy as making the decision to do so, and it makes a huge difference in the very moment we have given to it. And it makes an even bigger difference to the surrounding masses.

There is no thought any one of us has that doesn't affect every person on the planet.

There is no thought any one of us has that doesn't affect every person on the planet. This statement may seem outrageous, initially. But it is true nonetheless. Like perhaps some of you, I was skeptical at first. I had not heard about the butterfly effect, but as I encountered the idea, again and again, I knew it was a concept I had to investigate. Too many great minds believed in it for me to continue questioning it.

And now, I am relieved to say, I not only embrace this idea but stress it as a thought very worth thinking in every book I write and every workshop I offer. Now, that doesn't mean you have to accept it as true; but I do suggest you practice it and see how it changes the relationships in your life, and definitely take notice of how it influences your encounters with strangers, coworkers, even those people you aren't particularly fond of. You will be amazed.

Just for today, why not closely monitor every thought that comes to mind? Can you honestly say that it will bless those close at hand as well as those far away? Is it a thought you would be proud to shout in a public setting? If it isn't, how might you revise the thought before shouting it the second time?

This practice shows us exactly what we need to change. And the way to change isn't complicated at all. I can assure you. I did it—not always perfectly, but even doing it fairly well part of the time is making a worthy contribution to the planet we are sharing with so many suffering souls.

Perhaps you are wondering just what kind of thoughts might displease God. Of course I can't decide this for you, but I am always very aware of my attack thoughts. And I consider any judgmental thought an attack thought that would not be pleasing. I also consider those times when I am silently thinking anything negative about someone I know or even a complete stranger as something that would displease God. Displeasing thoughts aren't so subtle that I don't recognize them. Immediately, in fact. And just as soon as they are recognized I know I need to think something kind about the person standing before me.

This is such an easy behavior to address and correct that to not make an effort to do so is pretty unreasonable. In fact, I want to challenge you to make this difference in the lives of all seven billion people on this planet. We can benefit them all by allowing this single idea to become manifest in our lives, and not doing it is tragic, from my perspective.

Even practicing this for a day, for a morning, and then monitoring how you feel will convince you it is an idea that you can fully embrace. I feel like I can actually assure you that you will be more than mildly pleased if you take this challenge.

Revising your thoughts to be ones that would please God is an idea that's easy embraced. It's an idea that's easily fulfilled. And it's an idea that will change lives from this moment on. Are you willing to stand up and be counted? Seven billion people hope so.

Chapter 37

The hovering angels that never leave our side are giving us comfort and protection. Just look to them for your every need. Begin today.

The first time I read the epilogue following the lessons in the *Course in Miracles* workbook, I felt a shiver of hope, as strong an indicator as any I had ever experienced. That the hovering angels were a constant source of help required nothing more than for me to make the choice to believe in them. It was an easy choice. I had had an experience with an angel that pulled me away from the brink of suicide. Let me tell you about it.

I was in early recovery from alcoholism and drug addiction, a little more than forty-one years ago. I had perhaps eighteen months of sobriety at the time, and I had fallen into a very deep depression. I had been plagued by depression for much of my life and had been diagnosed as chronically depressed by my internist a number of years earlier, but I chose not to take medication to alleviate it. At that time, in AA rooms, medication of any kind for any ailment was frowned upon. In fact, many considered anyone on medication not sober. I was just too afraid to take what might have helped me at that time.

I fell into such a deep hole that I could imagine nothing better than dying to relieve the pain; so after not going to meetings, calling anybody for help, or teaching any of my classes (I was working on my PhD at the time and teaching at the University of Minnesota) for more than a week, I began the process of ending my life.

I took all of the towels I owned and rolled them up so I could stuff them in the windowsills in my one-bedroom apartment. I planned to then turn on the gas and just go to sleep. But God had another plan.

There was a loud rap at the door. I had not been expecting anyone, so I ignored it initially. Then I heard a voice call out, "Karen. Are you there?" At that, I went to the door and, barely opening it a crack, said, "Yes, I am here." This woman, a tall and very attractive redhead, said, "You made an appointment with me some time ago to talk over your finances."

I opened the door and she not all that politely pushed her way in. She said her name was Pat. I had never seen her before. She had her planner open and showed me my name. "See, this is our appointment. I am a busy woman, and I intend to keep my appointments."

I was stunned. Uninvited, she walked into my kitchen and sat down. When she looked at me, she asked, "Are you okay?" I told her I was a recovering alcoholic and was very depressed. I didn't mention my suicide plan. She made no comment about all the rolled towels. But her demeanor instantly changed. She softened and said, "My husband is an alcoholic. And I too have been depressed." And then she said, "I fully understand what you are experiencing. It has a name. It's called chemicalization. If you want to know more about it, look for Catherine Ponder's book, *The Dynamic Laws of Healing*."

She then went on to explain chemicalization's effects. She said I was on the precipice of a deepening spiritual breakthrough and my ego didn't want to let me move forward. It wanted to maintain its hold on me and keep me fearful. "The abyss you feel beneath you," she said, "will disappear as you reach out your hand and move toward God. He is waiting to bring you across." She spoke so softly, and with such certainty. I was both mesmerized and convinced that she spoke truth. And she said, "I envy where you are. I know what's waiting for you."

*"I envy where you are. I know
what's waiting for you."*

As quickly as she came, she got up to leave. Never were finances mentioned. I followed her to the door, and she turned back and put her arms out and gave me a warm hug. "You are going to be just fine. I am sure of it." And with that she was gone. A woman I had never seen before and never saw again. Was she an angel? I'm inclined to say yes. Wouldn't you be?

After her departure my depression lifted. I won't say I haven't struggled at other times over these four decades, but never quite like then. And now I know my angels are waiting to help. I simply need to acknowledge them. If you haven't allowed yours to help you yet, don't tarry. They know your needs. They have your answers. I feel pretty sure of that.

Making the decision to believe in angels
may not be an easy one for everybody. I
suppose there was a time I wouldn't have
been so easily convinced. But once they
come to your aid, you will never doubt
again. Give it a try. Won't you?

Chapter 38

Not one of the illusions you made replaces the truth.

How lucky for us that none of the illusions we have made at the hand of the ego replaces the truth, as shared with us by that other voice in our minds, the voice of the Holy Spirit. And what is that truth? There are many of them, actually, but one of them that's at the top of my list currently is the following: *Nothing real can be threatened. Nothing unreal exists.*

It is so easy to evaluate whether a person's words or deeds are representative of loving thoughts or appeals for healing or help. In other words, anyone we are in the presence of can be recognized pretty quickly. No one can mistake an expression of love. And certainly we all can recognize the harshness of judgment, or something far worse.

Nothing real can be threatened.
Nothing unreal exists.

But when the course tells us that the illusions, regardless of their content, are our egos' projections *and aren't real*, that indeed *they are illusory*, some of us balk at first. You can put me in that category. Even after years and years of study, I'd have to say that this is one of the hardest realities of the course to grasp.

This world we are walking around in certainly seems real. Even after being told I needed to think of it as a classroom for learning how to see differently, how to see all that's before us from a place of love rather than a place of fear, I was slow to be completely convinced. For a number of years I struggled to hang on to the truth that love, and only love in some form, was real. Everything else was a figment of my ego's projection. Everything.

What's most hopeful in this awareness now is my experience of seeking to see whatever is disturbing me from a different perspective. The mere act of seeking results in my willingness to see differently. And my willingness has made a huge difference in my relationships with many people.

It's certainly not uncommon for two people to see the same thing very differently. As a matter of fact, seldom do any two people agree completely on what lies right before them. But differing visions need not result in ugly disagreements. It often does, but it doesn't have to. When the ugliness rears its head is when one person needs to be humble enough to ask to see things differently. I can assure you that whenever I was *that person*, first a great sense of relief was felt throughout my body, which was always followed by a much-softened version of what I had seen before. The sense of relief was and is palpable every time, which makes the willingness to seek it easier with each attempt. As I said, *nothing real, within or without, can ever be threatened. And no illusion exists.*

Since I have been "walking the talk" for a lot of years now, I am able to say that practicing these principles has gotten easier. But it would be dishonest of me to say that I'm not capable of falling back into my old ego-directed behavior at least once every day. And some days, it's many more times than I really want to admit. However, let's focus on progress. Progress, not perfection.

If we catch ourselves even one time each day and allow the Holy Spirit to monitor and thus correct our remarks before we make them, we are adding benefit to the lives of others. It's as simple as being kind to everyone. And starting with the person standing next to us. That's what's real. That's not an illusion.

Sharing whatever we hear from the Holy Spirit, as well as what we hear from loving and kind companions, will always lead us gently into every situation, whether with family, friends, colleagues, neighbors, complete strangers, or even enemies. There is one way to be. One way to meet and greet the world of people who stand before us. Are you interested in bringing benefit to their lives? Just remember, any benefit you offer them benefits you tenfold.

Really, our journey is simpler than we
make it or even see it. One loving word
or thought at a time. One. And one
additional acknowledgment of what's
real, now and always.

Chapter 39

The separation never occurred.

N ever ever! Only in your ego mind did it occur, which is the creator of the entire illusory, extremely chaotic world. Only there was the separation even "thought" about. What the course so clearly tells us in passage after passage is that *we are still at home with God. We never left! God is in our minds, so leaving was impossible.* The ego has only made it appear that we did, taking all the control we will allow it to take to make ourselves miserable, living in a constant state of attack and fear. Seeing it everywhere. Projecting it everywhere. Thus, believing it is everywhere.

But there is the truth. The real truth. And the Holy Spirit knows it, has saved it for us, and willingly reveals it to us whenever we are inclined to listen to that softer voice within. We can't forget that the ego lives there too! We have a split mind, remember. And as the course says—as Jesus, in fact, said to Helen, the scribe of the course—"The ego speaks first. The ego speaks loudest. *And the ego is always wrong."*

How lucky you and I are that we decided to become students of *A Course in Miracles.* Nothing about your life or mine remains the same once we have decided to honestly absorb these ever so simple, frequently repeated but not so easily incorporated truths into our lives in order to walk among our fellow travelers with peace rather than agitation in our hearts. As I have said repeatedly, partly to reassure you but also to forgive me my failings, it doesn't matter that we can't practice peace every instant. Every time we do, it reverberates exponentially.

Let's go back to the main idea for this essay and explore it in greater detail. The separation between us and God, which this illusory world, a figment of the ego's imagination, has worked so hard to convince us of, simply has no reality. It never happened. We did not separate from God. Not really. We are still in the mind of God and God is still in our minds through the voice of the Holy Spirit. There is no separation. Not from Him. Not from each other. And this is one idea that sometimes needs additional explanation. For sure, I couldn't absorb it initially.

Indeed, it does seem we are separate from one another. I look across the room at you, and down at my body, and we don't appear to be one. This is a fact, however, that we finally have to take on faith, being willing that we will understand God's fuller message in due time. We are one because our true reality is Spirit. One Whole

Spirit that each of us is a part of. Once we make the decision to believe this on faith, your life, as my life, will feel freer, less stressful, certainly less agitated.

If I look across the room at you but see Spirit instead, see an expression of love instead, an expression that has actually come from me initially, the separation will exist no more. Agitation will exist no more. Fear, anger, and attack will exist no more. The point, obviously, is that it is up to us. Any change we want to experience has to be initiated by us. And when that change is to feel greater peace and love in your own life, the solution is terribly simple. Be the change. Be the change you want to see everywhere. Be the change you want to experience everywhere.

Be the change you want to see everywhere.

Be the expression of love. Be the purveyor of peace. Be the extension of kindness to everyone, all of those souls who seem so separate but are merely extensions of each of us, and all in spiritual partnership with God who has left not a one of us. *Not a one of us.* How impossible it may feel to even consider that this could be so. But it is. It is. Praise be to God.

Today will be as good as my willingness is
to see and be only love. The ego voice can
interfere, of course, but that's where we have
to double down and go into the mind once
again and wait for the softer voice to save us.
And the world around us.

Chapter 40

Our thoughts are all that can hurt us.

And, we can change them! In my life, before seeking recovery from alcoholism, codependency, and my need to control everyone and every situation around me (and the list could go on), I believed, honestly believed, that my thoughts simply happened to me, willy-nilly. I am a bit embarrassed to say I had never even considered that I, my mind, was the *actual* thinker.

When I eventually discovered that I had a split mind, which I wasn't to learn until I became a student of *A Course in Miracles*, I was treated to the idea that my thoughts could range from despicable, when the ego part of my mind was in charge, to overwhelmingly loving, when the Holy Spirit's voice was front and center. I was flummoxed, to say the least.

I hate to admit that even knowing about this split mind for more than three decades doesn't prevent me from allowing the ego part to have its say way too often. And its thoughts are never loving. Its thoughts are never kind. Its thoughts will never encourage me to be helpful, forgiving, circumspect, or beneficent. Its thoughts will see enemies everywhere, denying, in the process, that the ego part of my mind has projected everyone of them! And those thoughts will then encourage me to judge or, unfortunately, do far worse to all those projected "separate" people.

I'm not proud to admit my failings. However, I want you to remember that we are in a classroom and this is a process. A very long process. *A Course in Miracles* requires that we upend our entire former belief system. Discard it. And replace it. It was wrong. As Jesus said to Helen, the scribe, and I paraphrase: I have come again to explain what was misunderstood before [in the Bible]. Jesus wanted Helen, and thus all of us, to know that our journey is simply a pathway to love and its extension, and that we need to remove all the barriers to love that we have created. Period. Pretty simple, actually.

Why would we harbor thoughts that hurt us? Thoughts that are not loving. Why, indeed? The answer isn't mysterious, actually. It's habit. It's the old thought system that still has a tight hold on us. It's the ego that is part and parcel of that system. We are trapped in this collective nightmare created by the ego (that we students refer to as the classroom) to begin to remember who we really are: children of God who are still, *right now,* at home in the mind of God, a place *we never really left.* Amazing, isn't it?

Not everybody who turns to the course decides to stay on its path. It is radically different. Giving up our old thought system entirely seems too severe to many. However, for those of us who have taken the plunge, great freedom has visited us. Not daily, of course. My personal experiences shared throughout this book attest to that.

But today I have many moments free from those thoughts that can hurt me. And they used to be my only thoughts. And they did hurt. Unfortunately, they didn't hurt just me. Every thought I had I hurled at someone else, pretending it wasn't me who had it. That's what projection is all about. That's what the work of the ego is all about. "It's her, not me. Whew!"

There is a great line in the course that I love so much. And I think it's the answer to the dilemma of being released from the old, negative thought system. Just as a snake crawls out of its old skin, we too can shirk the old and move toward another perspective about life with a bit of help. And it comes. Jesus speaks to us and says in chapter 8, "The Journey Back," "If you want to be like me I will help you, knowing that we are alike. If you want to be different, I will wait until you change your mind."

"If you want to be like me I will help you, knowing that we are alike. If you want to be different, I will wait until you change your mind."

How kind. How loving. I had never ever considered asking Jesus for help of any kind. Seeking counsel with God was fine. Even believing, as I emphatically do as a student of *A Course in Miracles*, that the voice of the Holy Spirit in my mind has every answer that I need, turning to Jesus, who spoke so lovingly to Helen for more than seven years, giving her this document with the intention of reteaching us the truth and changing our lives completely, simply seemed foreign. My point is, there is no one voice we must listen to. *There is only one wrong voice.*

I would have to say I still seek the inner voice's message. And what surprises me is that I hear it. Not always in words. Sometimes in feelings or nudges. Sometimes in memories that resurface. It matters not; changing our thoughts, however works for us, is what we are attempting to do here. We need not harbor hurt. We need not foist hurt on others. There is another way to see. To live. To serve.

We can choose that other way.
Now. Let's make that difference.

Chapter 41

Remember that the Holy Spirit, the Voice, is the Answer, not the question.

This is an idea I have already put before you. From personal experience I know that any worthy idea needs many repetitions before it can be claimed as our own. And even then, unless we frequently use the idea in our daily living, it can slip away; not to be completely forgotten (no truth ever is), but it can be slightly inaccessible unless we quiet our minds and seek to know the truth once again.

Perhaps because of my age, or perhaps because of my many years of commitment to a journey more focused on love than fear, I am simply eager and willing to be as done as I can be with the machinations of the ego. Unfortunately, the ego, as many of you have experienced, is never eager to be done with us. It can be insistent. Unyielding.

Sometimes too powerful to be denied. But the voice will calm us if we let it. It's always our choice to let it.

The voice will calm us if we let it.
It's always our choice to let it.

It's always our choice to let it. I am soothed by that. It empowers me to be in charge of how I see the world around me. It empowers me to interact with the world in a kind, loving way regardless of how that illusion attempts to ensnare my ego. Let me assure you, I haven't forgotten that whatever snare is hurled my way is a projection that my ego, in fact, hurled out there. *What comes at us is of our own making.* A fact not easily acknowledged. Less easily accepted.

Don't be confused. If you are relatively new to the course, it's not easy to absorb all the workings of the ego, hear the voice of the Holy Spirit, and then be aware of and open to the tiny part in between the two voices that decides which one we will listen to. I have certainly not forgotten my early years of studying the course, sitting in study groups (which I highly recommend, by the way) and then coming home and rereading all that had been discussed, thinking maybe this time I will get it.

What I came to believe, with the help of many others along the way, including the great teachers of workshops who had been part and parcel of the entire unfolding of *A*

Course in Miracles from its very beginning, is that when I was ready to understand all that Jesus was telling me in the course, I would. And because he knew about resistance to the truth, something he had to overcome as well, he tells us, he comforts us by repeating the course truths again and again until they can become our own.

The title of this essay, "Remember that the Holy Spirit, the Voice, is the Answer, not the question" is one of those ever so significant truths that is presented to us over and over. You will come to know it. You will come to repeat it. You will come to treasure it just as I have. And, you will still forget it on occasion. That's the power of the ego. But the course is forgiving. We simply move on, knowing that in another moment we will have yet another opportunity to demonstrate our ability to let the voice urge us to say or do the next right thing. There will always be another opportunity. Always.

It may be that this particular truth has already been absorbed by you and gets frequent exercise. Bravo, if that's the case. You are bringing great benefit to many other souls sharing this planet with you. However, your work isn't done. The fact is, you and I are surrounded by others who haven't yet come to appreciate the importance of choosing the more peaceful path through the multitudes of encounters that occur, planet wide, on a daily basis. And just maybe we have an obligation to bring others along by our own example. Just maybe.

I have been personally thrilled to learn there is another way to navigate my journey *here*. Here in the illusion, that is. Before the course, even though I was committed to a twelve-step spiritual recovery, I was far too often listening to my ego. When the course finally called to me, I heard the real voice for another way to live for the first time. Being told there was another way to navigate through the trenches and among the many teachers so necessary to my journey has changed everything.

The last thought I want to leave with you here is that we will get to where we need to be when we need to be there. We are promised that. Don't fret. You will get the message you need on time. The voice will call. And you will be open to listening. That I know.

The voice of the Holy Spirit will never
leave us. Never. Our willingness to
listen is all that stands between us and
constant peace of mind.

Chapter 42

The Holy Spirit will take what the ego makes and transform it into a learning opportunity.

There isn't anything that the Holy Spirit can't transform into something helpful, perhaps even beautiful, and oftentimes the very experience that we have unknowingly needed for the life transformation we were destined to have. And we need not even be amazed. Whatever harm the ego tries to inflict—and I can certainly attest to its incessant, rigorous attempts—the Holy Spirit can not only undo the harm but transform it into something helpful.

Our lives feel complicated at times, or stressed; oftentimes we even feel unable to handle whatever is heading our way, certain that this time it may be beyond our capacity to withstand or understand. However, nothing will ever visit us—*nothing*—that with the Holy Spirit's help we can't handle. And whatever it is, it's headed our way by design. There are no accidents. There are no accidental encounters. Jesus has assured us of this. The Holy Spirit reaffirms it at every opportunity. We simply must decide to believe it. There is no better time than now, if you are still wavering.

There are no accidental encounters.

The ego doesn't ever speak the truth, remember. And the ego always speaks first, loudest, and with intent to do harm. It has no intention of allowing you to be at peace, in a state of blissful union with the other learning partners that have joined us here. To the ego, we are separate entities in constant conflict with each other and we're all hiding from God, who is out to destroy us because we escaped from our home with Him in Heaven.

The insanity of the ego's perspective can easily become our perspective too if we don't make the effort, even if we have to strain a bit, to hear the softer, gentler voice of the Holy Spirit. As you have read many times by now, although there is no communication ever between them, both voices reside in our minds. The choice we make about which one to listen to makes all the difference in every moment we experience.

Let's try a little experiment. Think about the most recent truly pleasant experience you had. Close your eyes a moment if that helps to block out all the static trying to get your attention. Can you remember what initiated the experience? Was it a call from an old friend? Maybe a son or daughter who doesn't check in all that often. Perhaps a compliment being paid in a very special way by a loved one. Or maybe it's something a bit further back in your memory that comes to mind. Why is it being reexperienced by you now as pleasant? What I'm driving at is we are constantly choosing how we interpret our lives. For sure, I said choose a pleasant experience. However, the ego can easily take whatever you focus on and twist it in a nanosecond into something very negative. Frankly, it sees that as its job.

If that didn't happen it was only because you made the decision to stick with the Holy Spirit's selection of a pleasant memory. I can assure you, the ego could have taken that memory and turned it into a: "But why did they wait so long to call?" or "I wonder why he didn't bring flowers rather than just a card?"

I said a bit earlier in this very essay, and as the title of this essay stipulates, the Holy Spirit will transform any ugly thought the ego has into something helpful, educational, and beneficial in some respect to the entire planet. The ego tries to do exactly the same thing, but in reverse. We must remain forever vigilant. Forever.

Quite assuredly, the Holy Spirit's capacity to make your life loving, peaceful, helpful to all others, and, at the end of the day, completely content is the gift God actually promised us when the Holy Spirit was given to us as His voice. And knowing that you have heard the right voice, you have followed the better suggestion, and you have added benefit, ultimately, to billions of learning partners sharing the journey is all the thanks one ever needs for a life well lived.

This path to greater peace that we have all chosen to walk is making a difference in the world at large. Perhaps we can't "see" that difference right now if we watch cable TV, but ever so slowly *A Course in Miracles*, coupled with many other similar peace-promoting pathways, are drawing adherents. And many spiritual leaders do believe that in combination *this collective* is moving toward that point of critical mass, a term borrowed from nuclear physics but defined here as that major shift in how travelers everywhere perceive this world and one another sharing it because of a chain reaction.

The change any one of us wants to experience begins with ourselves. We set an example by our actions and our words. And those actions and words will be a reflection of the voice we choose to listen to. It's truly not a hard choice. Not at all.

※

Who I present to the world today is by
choice. Will I, will we, move this vast group
of travelers toward that point of critical mass
where peace can finally reign supreme?

Chapter 43

The ego was made without love.
The Holy Spirit knows only love.

The title of this essay is succinct. And easily understood. *There is love and then there is the absence of love.* We must learn which way of seeing and therefore living we want to protect. The introduction to *A Course in Miracles* explains its purpose beautifully: "The course does not aim at teaching the meaning of love, for that is beyond what can be taught. It does aim, however, at removing the blocks to the awareness of love's presence, which is your natural inheritance."

"Love's presence is your natural inheritance" is a pretty strong statement. Let's ponder it a moment. Love is ours! We do not have to earn love. No one is excluded from love. No one. Nor can we escape love's presence. Unfortunately, we can refuse to acknowledge its presence, and that's the sole work of the ego. Daily, hourly, mean moment by mean moment, the ego is at work try-ing to thwart our awareness of love.

*Love is ours! We do not have to earn love....
Nor can we escape love's presence.*

To reiterate, why is the presence of love so hard to experience during many moments of our lives? Why have we put up blocks to that awareness of love? The answer will come to you, of course, but if you are still ponder-ing, let's remember what we have learned about the fierce, determined voice of the ego. Any moment you are feel-ing separate, alienated from others, afraid, unlovable, or unloving, you have been taken hostage by the ego. Being held hostage is not an aberration. It's one of the most eas-ily accomplished heists.

Fortunately, we can free ourselves from the long talons of the ego with a simple change of mind. And when we do, when we seek to hear that other voice, we will once again experience love. And we will wonder how we could ever have allowed ourselves to be bushwhacked by the ego. You are not unique. Everyone gets caught, some of us daily.

There's a sadness, I think, that the ego can never know love. Its entire being is fear. That's why it wants to make this body fearful too. It's his way of mattering. It's his way of taking charge. If he speaks loud enough, we will not be able to escape his demands. And he succeeds often, too often for many. But we must never give up or shut out the softer voice completely.

The course does stipulate in chapter 4, "The Illusions of the Ego," that "the ego can learn." It will never be able to communicate with Spirit. The two are forever uncommunicative. But both are present to our minds, our ears, our thoughts, our actions. When the thought or action suggested isn't loving, choose once again.

One of the first course teachers I studied with revealed, rather sheepishly, in one of our study groups that he had been exposed to *A Course in Miracles* a few years prior to his becoming an adherent and teacher. Like many of us, he was given the books (they were three separate volumes then) and attempted to read them. His ego fought him every step of the way until he gave up and put the books aside. Then one day he opened the text at random and the words "the ego can learn" caught his attention. Then and only then was he able to pursue the work that was to change his life—and through his teachings mine too, I might add.

I remain forever indebted to my friend George, who has left this illusion now. Because of him I developed a commitment to this study that will never die. It is as much a part of me as is my commitment to twelve-step recovery. Being able to see this "illusion" differently is my daily request to the Holy Spirit. Being willing to admit that it must be a daily undertaking is as necessary to me as my decision, made more than forty years ago, to never take that first drink again.

Having a daily spiritual practice is good for the soul. It's good for the others who travel with us to observe as well. We must not forget that we are the teachers of one another. Of course, this also means we are one another's students too. Being willing to live from a place of love, which is made possible if we listen to the soft suggestions of the Holy Spirit, is the example to others that will carry us home. Home to the home we never actually left. Our daily journey will allow us to fully understand this one day.

There is love and then there is the absence
of love. We can feel the emptiness when we
reside in the place where love feels absent.
Let's move into "the other realm," the
awareness of love, quickly. Just listen to the
softer inner voice.

Chapter 44

Our willingness to join with others reduces our fear and gives inner peace a chance—the peace that will eventually change this planet.

Always seeing others as separate from ourselves is certainly the work of the ego. Another aspect of the ego's work is its creation of fear as an ally, an ally that becomes central to all of us. This is not new information by now. I have presented this idea in many essays. But I'm reiterating it again here because of its paramount importance to the potential spiritual growth that awaits us all when we make the decision to listen to the other voice that's present in our minds.

What increases change in one of us, *any one of us*, eventually increases it in all of us. And the most important change we have to be willing to make is to give up our devotion to separateness, an aberration that has no truth to it when we surrender to the truth about who we really are, and become willing to embrace the idea of joining with others wherever they are. This book of essays has been written to cultivate that change.

The sense of separation that haunts any one of us occasionally, some of us nearly constantly, will truly disappear the moment we decide to seek a shift in perception. Let's review again how this shift happens. According to *A Course in Miracles, a miracle is nothing more than a shift in perception*, a shift away from "seeing" through the eyes of the ego to allowing the *vision* of the Holy Spirit to see for us.

We must ask to see differently. The shift
does not happen on its own.

Making that shift is not usually a single act. For most of us it's necessary to make the shift myriad times a day; for some, many times an hour even. And we must ask to see differently. The shift does not happen on its own. The good news is that we will never be denied the new perception when we have sought it. Never. I can vouch for this. It's perhaps the single most helpful tool I have employed over the more than thirty years I have been studying the course.

I can still recall the surprising relief I felt so many years ago when I first sought the help of the Holy Spirit to see a troubling situation differently. I had no real expectation that anything would be felt when I made the request. My spouse and I were having a disagreement over a stupid situation and we both had strong opinions—obviously strong egos too. I certainly didn't think any change in me or the circumstance would occur when, unknowingly to him, I silently made the request. Was I ever wrong! Immediately I felt lighter, looser, quieter. Immediately the disagreement no longer mattered to me. And what I gazed on looked and felt different too. I was gobsmacked, actually. We both just stopped and I silently smiled.

I have felt that same inner smile every time since when I have relied on this tool. What happens when you use it is that you no longer feel yourself as separate. You have allowed yourself to feel and be joined. You have allowed yourself to "see" Spirit within the other person. And it's in the joining of spirits that all healing occurs. That's exactly what we are seeking, with the help of the Holy Spirit, in this illusory world. We are seeking the truth of who we are. We are seeking to reconnect with our oneness.

Our fear simply dissipates about everything and everyone when we feel the oneness that is our truth. It's an amazingly simple transition once we commit to practicing it on a daily basis. And this practice changes us immeasurably if we allow it to. We do become the peace the planet deserves when we turn away from separateness and bond with Spirit as envisioned everywhere.

Being at peace within is very important to me. Having a quiet mind is very important to me. Having a sense of belonging wherever I go, having a sense of at-one-ment, regardless of which door I have opened or what group I have wandered up to, is what I am promised each and every time I rely on the tools of the course; in this instance, "Help me see this differently."

Serving as teachers to one another as we practice these tools is one of the assignments of our journey. Personally, I have grown to love that my life isn't just about me. And that your life isn't just about you. That we have a combined purpose, one that actually requires all seven billion of us eventually, is definitely a shift in my thinking. When I began this journey, I had no awareness of where I was headed. Now I can't imagine being on any other path.

It's amazing that you have joined
me here. Our oneness overwhelms me.
Our work is not yet complete, however.
Let's move forward together.

Chapter 45

As egos, we see
only what we want to see.

The ego is fully responsible for all the sights and sounds we experience in this illusory world. Every one of them. For instance, every other ego wrapped in a body, every circumstance that either entertains or angers us, and every situation that scares us are all by-products of one's ego. And it is always acting from a place of fear. Always. That is all it knows.

There is nothing in *this world* that is eternal, and that's the very proof that everything here is the ego's handiwork. Every tree dies, every blade of grass too. Every body is finally laid to rest. Absolutely nothing remains forever in the illusory world of the ego. Nothing unreal actually exists, remember.

Absolutely nothing remains forever in the illusory
world of the ego. Nothing unreal actually exists.

This is a very strong pronouncement, I know. Every aspect of what the ego is responsible for seems *too real not to actually be real*. This is one of the truths about the course's teachings that is hard, really hard for beginning students to grasp, I think. At least it gave me fits, on and off, for many of my early years as a student.

Everything we touch certainly seems real, doesn't it? Every person who walks toward us does too. Every sound we hear, along with every opportunity to pass judgment, or worse, can't just be a figment of my imagination. Can it? Unfortunately, yes, and we are so easily held hostage.

However, the course insists, gently but emphatically, that we eventually give up the thought system that so mistakenly creates and then controls the illusion that appears before us. Being told that we, as egos, have been harboring a thought system that is not only fallacious, suspicious, and capricious but also completely destructive and untrue is not very easy to believe. To some it seems impossible, initially.

Likewise, being introduced to a completely different, very loving, and rewarding thought system, opposite in every way, takes some getting used to also. How can two directly opposing thought systems exist? The answer is simple. Each one was created by *a force* who believed in it. And that force, the ego on the one hand and God on the other, are in the most important struggle we will ever experience: to claim us as its own messenger.

For our well-being, and the well-being of everyone around us, all seven billion of us, in fact, it obviously makes sense to be governed by the kinder, more loving thought system. But the ego's thought system does not give up easily. As I have said repeatedly, the ego speaks first, it speaks loudest, it always speaks from a place of fear, and it is never right. Or silent! And having grown accustomed to it, it's not easy to simply quit hearing it.

Our dilemma is a daily one. Which thought system we choose to embrace makes all the difference in what kinds of experiences we will encounter, and thus what kind of day we will have. The good news is that you can start your day over if you have mistakenly aligned yourself with the ego's thought system initially. As new course students, it is very common to have to choose again. Maybe many times a day. But there is no shame in having to make another choice because there is no shame in the thought system of the Holy Spirit.

As we grow accustomed to the course teachings, we can see how practical they are for our daily lives. That is the very reason I have remained an uncompromising adherent all these many decades. I want practicality. I want to see peace instead of *this*. I love the experience of seeing Spirit in my sisters and brothers instead of the ego chaos my own ego is capable of hurling out there. Perhaps I should say I am tired of the merry-go-round of negativity the ego creates. Maybe you are becoming tired too.

There is a solution for our weariness. Make another choice. Make the choice to listen to the Holy Spirit rather than the ego and your heart will feel full, your mind will experience the stillness of peace, you will see Spirit present in your brothers and sisters, and you will know that all is well.

How sweet it is to know that all is well. We
can rest in that place moment by moment
when we listen to the voice of God, which
comes to us from the Holy Spirit. Let's listen.

Chapter 46

Christ's vision allows everyone who is willing to see others without judgment.

There is a process that can trigger our willingness to give up our judgments of others. When we just say "I am going to quit judging others," we often fall short. Probably more truthfully, we mostly fall short. However, there is no shame in our failure. Even repeated failures. The ego is hard at work and its sole intent is to make us see through the eyes of fear, which puts judgment on a pedestal. Its success is all too evident when we pause, for even a moment, and listen to talk radio or watch cable news.

And as we compulsively look with judgment on other egos, as we are so accustomed to doing, we are told by the Holy Spirit to simply notice what our egos have done once again, *simply notice*, and then quietly move on. Remember, what's out there mirrors what's in here. How gently we are treated by the Holy Spirit. Never judged. Never shamed. Never denied. That's the crux of the process: repeated attempts to quit judging followed by repeated forgiveness experiences with the Holy Spirit.

The Holy Spirit sees as Christ sees. They have a shared vision. In other words, they see through forgiving eyes only. When it comes to egos seeing other egos without judgment, it obviously means seeing them, with the help of the Holy Spirit or Christ, as forgiven. As always, already forgiven. We must begin to see ourselves that way too, of course, since whatever we see "out there" is what our egos hurled out there for us to see.

Don't let the interchangeable terms of the Holy Spirit and Christ confuse you as they did me initially. The Holy Spirit is our communication link to God. Oftentimes the link is referred to as a bridge in the course. Whatever we hear from the Holy Spirit is what God has chosen for us to hear.

Christ also represents that link to God, who is still in the Kingdom. Seeing from our spirit into the spirit of others is seeing the face of Christ everywhere. And that means there is no fear to feel, no anger to address, no judgment that makes us feel ashamed when we invite ourselves to see Christ in the faces of the egos we have arranged to meet on this journey. Freedom from the brutal vision of the ego is so refreshing, so hopeful, so quieting.

All we have to do to transition from seeing as we have always seen to seeing truth is to pose the question, "Help me see this/him/her differently." And help is received. Instantaneously! Our world is righted when we seek the help that can upend the old thought system.

What a gift we have been given by Jesus, who shared his healed thoughts with Helen Schucman, the course's scribe. And what a debt of gratitude we owe her for sitting quietly in her study, night after night for seven years, taking down his every thought in shorthand, and not one of them did she embrace during the process. Not one. However, she did come to believe in Jesus as a friend and way-shower.

There is a great story in Schucman's biography, *Absence from Felicity*, written by Kenneth Wapnick, who was her very good friend. Wapnick was the editor for the course, and he wrote many additional books about its meaning too. He was an exceptional teacher as well.

When the student is ready, the teacher will appear.

The story Wapnick shares is so touching: he often went shopping with Helen simply because she asked him to. They admired each other greatly. And on one occasion, she desperately needed green nylons for a particular dress she wanted to wear on a special occasion. They looked and looked, going in one store after another. And then she remembered she should ask Jesus for his help. Need I say more? He immediately directed her to the store and the clerk who was to help her. She purchased the nylons without even a thought that others might think this turn of events rather odd.

You recall, I'm sure, that Jesus promised us in the text of *A Course in Miracles* that whatever he had been able to do we could do also, on this marvelously peaceful pathway that is changing every one of us, making us truly one, when we are ready.

Depending on the distance you have traveled already on this spiritual journey, you may be more ready than some, or as yet not as willing as others, to believe how like Jesus you really are. It matters not where you are on this timeline. In the Real World time doesn't exist anyway. It will happen when it happens. I, for one, simply no longer doubt. And that pleases me.

Some years ago, I surrendered to the realization that many course ideas were difficult to fully grasp, at least as completely as I figured they needed to be eventually grasped. And then it hit me. Every idea I struggled with got repeated in a bit different form dozens and dozens of times, and each time I encountered it, it became a bit more available to my mind. *When the student is ready, the teacher will appear.*

Go easy on yourself as you move through the course, trying to absorb this complete reversal of your previous thought system. Go easy. It will come.

Chapter 47

The Holy Spirit translates
the laws of God.

W e are so fortunate to have this constant help from the Holy Spirit—if we choose it, that is. No one has forgotten, I'm sure, how incessantly the ego calls out to us to listen to its translations. And listening to the ego will never offer us the quiet, peaceful guidance we truly deserve. Those around us truly deserve our patronage of the Holy Spirit too.

What comes to us from the Holy Spirit is direct from God. The Holy Spirit is the bridge to the Kingdom, the home of God and our real home too. We have simply forgotten, for a time, who we really are and where we really live. The Holy Spirit is present to gently remind us. And the ego feels in direct competition, even though the two voices are never in direct communication with each other.

The ego's survival rests on our listening to it and letting its perception become our perception too. It's an ugly perception, however. It sees enemies everywhere. It runs on fear, and if we listen to it we run on fear too. If only it didn't speak first, so very loud, and incessantly. Alas, that's how it sees its job. If we want a quieter life, we simply have to turn toward the Holy Spirit, allowing its voice to calm us and guide us to expressions of love.

Obviously you are seeking a quieter, more peaceful journey or you would not have been inspired to pick up this book. I, too, was seeking a quieter, more peaceful journey when I "just happened" upon the course. I was searching but I didn't know for what. I struggled to find a consistent connection to God. I observed others doing it but couldn't find it myself. My struggle drove me to the brink of suicide after being sober a bit more than a year. And then I felt the connection.

Unfortunately, my connection remained intermittent for some time; and then the tide began to turn ever so slightly. It has been turning pretty consistently ever since. And the primary explanation I have for the turn is my thirty-year study of *A Course in Miracles*. Like I said, I "just happened" upon it, but I don't honestly believe that for a moment. My so-called discovery was part of my divine journey all along. And my sister-in-law who sent me the books was obviously part of the plan too.

Learning to rely on the availability of the Holy Spirit's guidance is what has truly made my life sweeter. And that's absolutely my hope for you as you have pondered the many essays here. I simply want us all to appreciate what peace feels like. For sure, if we allow our minds to be eaten up by the harangue of the ego's voice, we will not know peace. Ever!

The reason it is hard to always be in tune with the Holy Spirit is because our minds can become so easily conflicted in a nanosecond. We awaken, read our lesson or devotional of some kind for the day, sit quietly for a few minutes with the God of our understanding, and then turn on the news just to see what has transpired overnight. And the ego has nabbed us once again. Chaos reigns. The conflict is ever present. But we can choose once again, and for the health of ourselves, and the peace of all those individuals we will pass on our journey today, make your choice carefully.

Don't fret if you find yourself back in the clutches of the ego almost immediately. That's the power of the ego. The Holy Spirit is far more powerful, however. It just waits quietly for us to turn to it. Let's not tarry with the ego for long. It offers us nothing good. Not now. Not ever. And the Holy Spirit, the extension of God directly to us, offers us only love.

Every loving thought is true; everything else is an appeal for healing and help, regardless of the form it takes.

Let me repeat one of the Holy Spirit's primary lessons: every loving thought is true; everything else is an appeal for healing and help, regardless of the form it takes. The constant application of this lesson will change every moment of the rest of your life. I can promise you this. I can also promise you that the ego isn't gone. It is pernicious, suspicious, and vicious. The choice you will need to make often is your salvation.

It's a real blessing that even though the ego brought us on this wild goose chase, creating this illusory world that keeps us constantly off balance, certain that it could create better than God, and, as the text tells us, "we forgot to laugh," so here we are. But with patience we are finding our way to sanity, one moment at a time, if we are willing to listen to God's interpreter.

Making the choice for God, as shared
with us by the Holy Spirit, promises
peace. If you are struggling to make
this choice today, try again. Now.

Chapter 48

To have peace we must teach it.
Only then do we learn it.

C hanging how we understand truth is what this essay is about. And one of the truths of *A Course in Miracles* is that to have peace we must teach peace; and in the process, learn peace more completely too. Vigilance is the key word.

It's probably not new information that we learn more about who we are and what we believe every time we share a thought with someone else. Sharing thoughts about choosing the peaceful life makes our desire for the peaceful life grow in intensity. Thus, we learn what we share. Our belief in peace grows as we share our beliefs with others.

What does it mean to teach peace? I think the best way to teach it is to show, by example, what peace looks like. We do this through our demeanor. Through the choice of words we use. Through our kindnesses toward others. And we do it best when we refrain from entering into the chaos that others invite us to join.

Talking about peace has its place too, but we have all known folks who talk the talk but fail to walk the walk. Being a pure example of peace is the best teaching, of course, but it's not all that easy. However, even being an occasional example of genuine peace does not go unnoticed. What is also noticed is the person who speaks about peace but never treats others kindly.

Making the decision to change our own life first is the obvious step we need to take. And it's not as difficult as it may appear to be initially. How do we grow in our understanding of what peace looks like? What works best is to turn to the Holy Spirit, who is always present and only a thought away. Remember, He is sharing our mind with the ego. They are not preaching the same tune, however. Their messages are diametrically opposed to each other.

It's about choice. Do we really want to be more peaceful? Do we really want to help others choose this path too? If we can agree to both ideas, there is only one thing to do. Listen first and always to the Holy Spirit. Its voice, its message, is coming directly from God. *Directly from God.* It can't get much clearer than that. And all we have to do to get God's message, to get that encouragement to be an example of peace, is seek it.

All we have to do to get God's message, to get that encouragement to be an example of peace, is seek it.

Our lives in these bodies, in this illusory dream, can be far quieter, more pensive, more loving, and for sure more peaceful. Just because we are in this classroom doesn't prevent us from seeking a sweet dream rather than accepting the nightmare of chaos the ego prefers we live in. Making the choice to refrain from allowing the ego to make any decisions for us is the first major decision we need to make. It has no good suggestion for you. None. Stay away from that choice if you want to experience the joy you deserve.

Vigilance. It's about vigilance. If we want to become the loving person our pet thinks we are, it's probably time to make some changes. Not one of the changes is too difficult for any one of us. Actually, we have been changing in large and small ways all our lives. But for some of us, the biggest change may be on the horizon. And because you have selected to read this book, that may be the indication you are ready for the plunge that will make your life all you hoped it would ever be.

I know I spent a lot of years in the chaos, not knowing there was another way to live. I can still slip into it if I turn on cable news. But the quiet mind cultivated by the Holy Spirit draws me so much more easily these days. I know you will find that to be true for you too. Practice. Practice and vigilance create the turning point for our lives.

I had no idea when I began the study of the course so many years ago that I would be exchanging my entire thought system for one that makes so much more sense to me. And I couldn't be happier. Living from a place of love rather than a place of fear calls to me every day now. Not every day am I completely successful, but I know there is always another day and many more opportunities to choose once again.

The decision to teach peace is a worthy one—one that reaches far more than just those individuals on your path today. What you do now affects the planet. Make the right choice, won't you?

Chapter 49

God did not leave us comfortless even though we "chose" to leave Him and our home in Heaven.

W hat a sweet reminder. We have not been left without comfort. Regardless of the insanity that created the so-called escape from the Kingdom and our home with God, we have not been forgotten. We have not been forsaken. As a matter of fact, we have been given a direct line of communication with God through His gift of the Holy Spirit, who has taken up residence in our minds, sharing that special place with the ego, the culprit that started all the chaos and led us on this wild goose chase into this illusory nightmare.

What a difference that can make in every moment of our lives when (and this is a big when) we remember to rely on the Holy Spirit for guidance rather than the insane attack guidance we will always get from the ego. Even though there is no communication between the Holy Spirit and the ego, since both voices reside in our minds, we have to choose carefully which one we think can give us what we need to know, what we need to think, and what we need to do.

It's good practice, actually, to sit quietly before making any choice about who to listen to and then what action to take. There will be occasions, particularly early on in this journey to a new way of seeing, that we will listen to and then follow the suggestions of the ego. We are on a steep learning curve. We need not feel ashamed of making the wrong choice, even when it's more than occasionally at first. The ego is demanding. The Holy Spirit quietly awaits our nod.

The wonderful realization is that we discover, after making that nod a few times, that our lives feel so much more peaceful when we turn to the comfort of God, comfort that the Holy Spirit will always supply. Always. The nod is such a simple gesture, isn't it? And it's a great exercise too, not only toward the Holy Spirit but toward all the travelers we meet on our daily journey. A simple nod of acknowledgment lets them know we have witnessed their presence, one of the kindest gifts we can quietly offer another person.

That same nod to the Holy Spirit opens the door to a gift being received from Him to us, a gift of love that we in turn can then express, can extend to others. What we get from the Holy Spirit will immediately add benefit to the planet we share with so many others, *as long as we extend it*. Extending it feels so good. It joins us with our companions, those who have, with intention, shown up.

When I remember that the Holy Spirit's primary direction to us, a direction that comes from God, the Father, is to lovingly join with all others, I feel such peace. Such comfort. To refrain from seeing ourselves as separate, as frequent adversaries, which is a fallacy anyway except in this illusion, is a beautiful awareness.

Another comforting step, of course, which is another gift from God to us through the Holy Spirit, is to seek to see the face of Christ in our companions. Let me reiterate the importance of this truth: We are not separate human beings. We have erroneously been convinced of that by an insane ego who knows nothing that is true. Nothing.

We are not separate human beings. We have erroneously been convinced of that by an insane ego who knows nothing that is true. Nothing.

For some of you, this is a new journey. *A Course in Miracles* is a new direction, a whole new endeavor. I am delighted that you have joined the millions of us who have already chosen this path to freedom. And it is a path of freedom. Freedom from anger. Freedom from attack thoughts. Freedom from alienation. Freedom from the sense of loss that came when we allowed the ego to take us on the journey into chaos.

There is a way back to our home. Turn to the Holy Spirit for comfort and guidance and you will be at home, and at peace, while still in this classroom of chaos. Our journey is a process. Keep wrapping the comfort of the Holy Spirit around you and you will lovingly serve as the teacher you are here to be.

We have a mission here in the classroom.
Fortunately, we do not have to guess about how
to fulfill it. We have all the guidance we really
need. Let's seek it. The Holy Spirit is waiting.

Chapter 50

No call to God will ever be unheard or unanswered.

This promise to us is absolute. No call will ever be unheard or misplaced. And even more importantly, unanswered. God is present to us every moment. Whether we feel present to God or not. I love being reminded of this. There were many years in my life, particularly in my early recovery from addictions, that I had no sustained awareness of God at all. I couldn't seem to find Him or feel Him in spite of many others assuring me of His presence. Learning, as I have, that God still had an awareness of me every moment, regardless of my not being aware of Him, is a very sweet fact. One that I cherish very much.

And I believe this sweet fact now without reservation. And it's my hope you will believe it too. Being promised this from Jesus, who shared it with Helen, and then, from her to us, is a promise we need never doubt. Just make a call and see what happens.

I think that when we feel a call isn't being heard, it's because we aren't waiting quietly enough for the answer. Or maybe it's because we had an answer in mind already that we preferred, one perhaps supplied by the ego, and so we didn't hear what we actually needed to hear when it was offered.

When we are faced with a dilemma of any kind, we don't even have to formulate a very specific question. We can simply say, "Help."

When we are faced with a dilemma of any kind, we don't even have to formulate a very specific question. We can simply say, "Help." And then sit quietly while God works it out. What will happen, absolutely, is that a nudge, at the very least, will be felt. Perhaps a nudge to call a friend who is going to amazingly make a comment that answers our call for help. Or perhaps we take notice of a book on the counter, one we had meant to put away, opened to a particular page; and before closing it we see where we had underlined a few sentences sometime in the past, now long forgotten. And those words are just what we were seeking.

Does it mean that because we didn't hear an exact message from God through the Holy Spirit that we were being ignored? On the contrary. We weren't being ignored. Our answers did come. And they always will. We simply have to believe in that promise and seek to see the answers however they present themselves.

Perhaps some of you are still not certain *A Course in Miracles* is a path you feel called to with the same devotion that I have developed over these last three decades. And that's perfectly okay. We come to a new way of seeing and thinking when we are ready. There is not a timeline. There are those who believe we will all join this path in time, however. That matters not to me. What I want for you is peace of mind. And that's what turning to at least some of the fifty-two course principles that I've presented here will offer you, I hope.

Nothing has become more important to me in my advancing years than feeling at greater peace. I believe with such certainty that my extension of peace and my offering of love and forgiveness to others is what changes me. And the course tells me this is what changes the world around me as well.

When I am seeing the face of Christ in the others around me, when I am offering them a sign of peace, when I am allowing my heart to overflow with love for them, be they strangers or friends, I know I have joined with the one whom I have projected before me. And that's how healing happens. That's how oneness is achieved. That's how truth is expanded.

If you are still slightly on the fence about this path, perhaps just taking a small bite for now is enough. I had to take it slow at first. I couldn't get my mind around the idea of a reversal of my entire thought system. But it has happened. And with little effort on my part. Willingness to consider there might be a better way and then committing to seeking it is what I became open to.

As I've said, my desire for peace finally exceeded my desire for winning any argument. That's what helped me turn my corner. Maybe that will help you too.

Trusting that God will answer every call is the first necessary step. For some, it may take a while. No rush. Keep trying. The Holy Spirit will always give you His answer.

Chapter 51

We do not walk alone.
God's angels are hovering all
around us, now and forever.

How comforted I am every week when our study group reads the epilogue at the end of the course workbook. It begins:

This course is a beginning, not an end. Your friend goes with you. You are not alone. No one who calls on Him can call in vain. Whatever troubles you, be certain that He has the answer, and will gladly give it to you, if you simply turn to Him and ask it of Him.

Being reminded that we are never alone, that "God's angels hover near and all about," fills me with a warm glow of God's love and peace that is palpable. Actually, each week there are multiple sighs from group members because the assurance we are given, though no longer doubted, warms our hearts again anyway. There are some things we simply can never hear too often.

The idea of angels hovering around us may be a stretch for some people who are new to *A Course in Miracles*. But I would have to say, when I read that paragraph even the very first time more than thirty years ago, it took ahold of my mind and heart in a way I had not expected nor ever experienced. I no longer remember if I believed in angels as a youngster, but I do know that I scoffed at the idea of angels in my early adulthood. No more. Absolutely no more.

And now I find the very thought of them a sweet addition to the comfort I seek from the Holy Spirit while still experiencing the insanity of this classroom created by the ego. I have journeyed a long time "here" now. How much longer the classroom will claim me is still beyond my comprehension, but I do know, from constant experience, that every time I seek the guidance of the Holy Spirit, I am transported away from the nightmare and into a *sweet dream*. And the more often I seek the sweet dream, the more willing I am to see myself as joined with, never separate from, those who travel here too.

Finally, I have grown comfortably convinced that in regard to my own life, the journey in this classroom has been for these specific purposes: to change how I understand and then embrace forgiveness, to change how willing I am to experience and extend love, and to heighten my awareness of peace and appreciation for what it can do, not only for me but for every life that I touch.

If we can't bring good into the communities we live in and visit, what really is the reason for our presence anywhere? We have the capacity to make such a difference in the lives of our brothers and sisters, those people we have scorned as our enemies, rather than seeing them as our own ego projections. The time to make a difference is now. Help is available to make that difference. The Holy Spirit has the answer to the disease of separation that our egos have caused. The decision to see us joined as one, whole and holy, is only a moment away.

The decision to see us joined as one, whole and holy, is only a moment away.

There really is no kinder, more loving decision we could make right now, at this very moment, than to choose to hear the voice of the Holy Spirit, who can correct for us any error in thinking our egos have made. And following that, He will give us the thoughts and words and actions that will help all of our journeymen experience the sweet dream too that we all deserve.

Let's never forget that when the ego was made, as the result of "a tiny mad idea," chaos began to reign in the classroom. However, God gave us the call to joy. Joy will always drown out the ego's call to attack if we allow it to, if we make the better choice.

It all comes down to choice. What kind of experience do you want to have? Do you want to live a peaceful journey, and perhaps teach others to also choose peace as a way to live? Or do you want to stay stuck in the trenches of chaos with the ego making your decisions?

It's my guess that you wouldn't have gotten nearly to the end of this book if you didn't want something to change in your life. Perhaps I have helped you make a few of those changes. But remember, we have all the time we need to make changes. And every choice we make can be remade if we aren't content with the outcome.

Let me remind you what it says so beautifully very early on in the text:

I am here only to be truly helpful.

I am here to represent Him Who sent me.

That's the most loving assignment each of us is invited to undertake. To be truly helpful. Wholly helpful. Lovingly helpful. And the hovering angels are constantly present to help us fulfill the assignment. This I know for certain.

※

Wait not a moment more; invite the hovering
angels to help you see peace everywhere you
look, and your life will change forever. Mine
did. And they will never leave our side.

Chapter 52

You will be told what God wills for you each time there is a choice to make. Go in peace from this moment on.

E ven though this is your final essay, it's likely your transformation has only just begun. We get as much time as we need, however, to remember who we really are. We have been held hostage by the ego since waking up in this classroom, this illusion that thankfully gives us an opportunity, each and every moment, to reclaim the truth of who we are. We forgot that truth when we made the choice to deny that we were One; that we were the child of God; that we were still in Heaven, our home, with God.

What a silly mad idea the ego conjured up. But that idea held sway, and here we are, in this seemingly faraway classroom, being bombarded by a voice that preaches insanity, anger, attack ideas, and evil; and we strain to hear the other voice that also calls to us. Fortunately, that other voice will never disappear. Never. It will wait for us to tire of the chaos.

Becoming tired of the chaos is an individual matter. Some tire of it quickly. Some wallow in it for years. All we have to do is pick up a newspaper or an iPhone and we get evidence of the millions of adherents to chaos, and we see, too, how desperately they try to engage the rest of us to join the insanity. Even after making the choice to listen to the quieter voice that speaks to us of love and kindness, we can occasionally become ensnared. And then we have to remember, all over again, that this world is a classroom, and our real assignment is to remember who we really are. And to remember, for all those who have forgotten, how to find the way back to sanity. To God. To Heaven. Home.

This world is a classroom, and our real assignment is to remember who we really are.

It's my hope that you have found comfort and solace through these essays. Many of the ideas were repeated, in some form, myriad times. That was by intention. We seldom remember with ease that which is new to us. This, coupled with the incessant voice of the ego, who "causes us to disremember" that which will bring joy to our lives, requires more than just a bit of repetition. At least that has been my experience.

It is my hope that you have discovered the way to peace and joy, the way to forgiveness and wholehearted love, requires nothing more than a simple decision—a decision that can be made and remade as many times as necessary until you remember who you really are in this classroom, a classroom that screams pain and fear, anger and attack, alienation and hopelessness. There is another way. And that way has been outlined for you, over and over. Simply pause and seek to hear the quieter voice, the voice of the Holy Spirit, who has been directed by God to help you find your way back home and to help you serve others in their journeys too.

Any worthy idea bears repeating. And there is really no more worthy idea than the promise that you will be told what God wills for you each time you doubt what your next move, your next thought, your next action should be. Your only need is to make the choice to listen. And you can take as long as you need to make that choice. God is not going anyplace. Not ever. He lives within, now and forever.

To walk in peace with a heart filled with love is
my opportunity today. It's your opportunity too.
Shall we be the difference this planet needs?

Concluding Thoughts

I have shared so many thoughts with you throughout these fifty-two essays that you might be wondering, why more? I'm sure you also noted the often-repeated thoughts I selected as so important for transforming how we see our lives, and thus live them. They were not just random selections I chose to repeat. They were the specific ideas that have moved me to a new way of seeing. A way that has truly transformed my life.

Every single idea I selected, and many more too, of course, came directly from Jesus to us through Helen Schucman, the scribe. She coherently wrote down each word she heard, night after night, for seven years. In shorthand. It was those very messages that became *A Course in Miracles*, a 1,249-page book that has been translated into more than twenty-five languages since it was first published in English in 1975. It was those very messages she shared with the world that have changed my life completely, and millions of other lives too.

It's been my intention, and in all honesty my goal, to impart to you some of those ideas that have impacted my life so deeply these last three decades. I think this intention isn't unusual, actually. Whenever we are struck by an idea that speaks loudly to us, that moves us to a higher spiritual awareness and then changes us for the better, don't we want to share it with friends? That's always been true for me. I hope you know that even though we may have never met, I do consider you my friend, and my companion for sure, on this journey to peace.

It's quite possible that you are a far quicker study than I was, but I needed a great deal of repetition of these remarkable ideas before I could actually claim them as my own. I made the assumption that the same might be true for you. If I have erred here (and that's surely possible) and the repetition has burdened you—or worse, bored you— please forgive me; and as we say in twelve-step rooms, "Take what fits and leave the rest." No harm intended.

My multiple references to the Holy Spirit, that direct link in our minds to God and our real home, whose voice is always soft and always filled with loving suggestions for us and our brothers and sisters; all those references to the ego, the always brash, always loud voice who is *always* wrong and whose sole intention is to make our lives a living nightmare; and finally the references to some select, very specific course truths were all made with careful consideration for how best to help you as I had been helped. I surely hope I have succeeded.

We are embarking on an entirely new way of seeing and thinking in this study that you and I have undertaken. In fact, as we are told in the course text itself, these ideas represent a thought system that is directly opposite to the thought system most of us have sworn allegiance to prior to coming to *A Course in Miracles*. That's a huge change for most of us. And big changes generally can't be absorbed except incrementally. I have tried to offer these ideas in an incremental fashion. Again and again. Over and over. Hopefully I have met with success.

Finally, I want to share some thoughts about why writing this particular book has been so important to my journey. As you will recall, my path to the course followed my journey into twelve-step rooms more than forty years ago. In fact, my first twelve-step meeting was in the fall of 1974, which was followed by my joining AA in 1976. And once a twelve-stepper, always a twelve-stepper has been my motto. I have adopted *A Course in Miracles* with as much relish. I am quite positive I will study the course, enthusiastically, and most likely in a study group, for the rest of my life. My memory is simply too short to remember the way to peace without being reminded of the simple plan that has been laid out by Jesus in the text and the workbook.

A word about Jesus. Perhaps some of you may be reacting much like I did when I first became a student. I knew the messages had come to Helen from Jesus, and I felt comfortable with most of them; but then I more or less blocked Jesus from my mind. Why? I can't answer that. I think I recoiled from the idea that Jesus speaking sounded too Christian fundamentalist. And then, after reading Helen's biography, I had a different feeling for Jesus. And I appreciate her for that. I know he was just like me originally, and then he fulfilled his journey, the same one we are making.

Why is peace paramount in my life now? I think partly because of my age. In my youth, being right was paramount. Even well into adulthood, being right, being first, being chosen all ranked way ahead of being peaceful. And none of those things even make it to the list of what's important anymore. None of them. And I don't even find that curious.

We do change as we age. We do begin to see our lives from a different perspective. And choosing to adopt *A Course in Miracles* as an additional safety net while I continue my search for blissful peace has made such sense. And actually, that's enough to satisfy me.

I wanted to bring you gently along to considering a new way of seeing the world around you. I wanted you, throughout the book, to understand that miracles were only a thought away. And the most significant way to access one was merely to pose the question, "Help me see this differently." We are guaranteed a new vision when we seek one. Additionally, I know from thousands of requests that the Holy Spirit never denies even one. Never.

I also hope I have helped translate some of the course truths in a way that has made them accessible and acceptable to you. Sharing what I have learned with you has helped me. My learning curve continues. I was so gladdened by learning that the Holy Spirit was assigned, by God, as a translator for us. Having a personal guide has meant so much. I have tried to serve you as a guide too.

I have never meant to be pushy in any of the guidance I have shared in the essays. If it ever felt that way, forgive me. I simply feel time is running out. The world we are sharing with billions of other suffering souls needs as many examples of peace as we can willingly model. All I have wanted to do here is interest you in being one of those models and giving peace a chance.

I do hope you will choose to read through the book a second or third time, if you are so moved. I never intended for it to be read quickly and only once. My only plan here was to serve as a guide and share, through my own life experiences, that change is possible. Peace is possible. Love for everyone—everyone—is possible. That's an *educated* promise. However, I did learn to rely on the hovering angels, who I firmly believe surround us always, to help me stick to my agenda: be an expression of love regardless of whom I meet on the journey each and every day. Perhaps you will seek their help as well.

And finally, may your journey, day in and day out, fill you with love. May it bless you in untold ways. And may you be willing to pay forward what you have received by loving and blessing at least one traveler on your path each day too.

May we meet again in some peace-filled moment.

I am so fortunate that Red Wheel/Weiser and Conari Press took an interest in being my publisher more than a decade ago. Jan Johnson, a friend and former colleague, said yes when I offered her a book. I haven't yet been told no, and for that I am very grateful. I have had the good fortune to be shepherded by some wonderful folks there, Caroline Pincus for one, Jane Hagaman too. And last but not least, Greg Brandenburg, who has now inherited me. I consider myself truly lucky to be in such good and capable hands all these many years.

I hope you all know you have a special place in my heart. And you always will.

About the Author

KAREN CASEY is a writer and workshop facilitator for 12-step recovery. Her first book, *Each Day a New Beginning*, has sold more than 2 million copies. She has published 28 books since then including *Change Your Mind and Your Life Will Follow*, which was a finalist for the MS Society Books for a Better Life Awards. She has traveled throughout North America and Europe carrying her message of hope for others on the road to recovery.

Visit her at *www.womens-spirituality.com*.

To Our Readers

Conari Press, an imprint of Red Wheel/Weiser, publishes books on topics ranging from spirituality, personal growth, and relationships to women's issues, parenting, and social issues. Our mission is to publish quality books that will make a difference in people's lives—how we feel about ourselves and how we relate to one another. We value integrity, compassion, and receptivity, both in the books we publish and in the way we do business.

Our readers are our most important resource, and we appreciate your input, suggestions, and ideas about what you would like to see published.

Visit our website at *www.redwheelweiser.com* to learn about our upcoming books and free downloads, and be sure to go to *www.redwheelweiser.com/newsletter* to sign up for newsletters and exclusive offers.

You can also contact us at *info@rwwbooks.com.*

Conari Press
an imprint of Red Wheel/Weiser, LLC
65 Parker Street, Suite 7
Newburyport, MA 01950
www.redwheelweiser.com